Primary School A[ssemblies]
for Religious Festi[vals]

Edited by Ronni Lamont

First published in Great Britain in 2012

Society for Promoting Christian Knowledge
36 Causton Street
London SW1P 4ST
www.spckpublishing.co.uk

Copyright © SPCK 2012

The authors of the individual assemblies included in this work have asserted their rights under the Copyright, Designs and Patents Act, 1988, to be identified as such.

All rights reserved. No part of this book may be reproduced or transmitted in any form or by any means, electronic or mechanical, including photocopying, recording, or by any information storage and retrieval system, without permission in writing from the publisher.

SPCK does not necessarily endorse the individual views contained in its publications.

The authors and publisher have made every effort to ensure that the external website and email addresses included in this book are correct and up to date at the time of going to press. The authors and publisher are not responsible for the content, quality or continuing accessibility of the sites.

Unless otherwise noted, Scripture quotations are taken from the New Revised Standard Version of the Bible, Anglicized Edition, copyright © 1989, 1995 by the Division of Christian Education of the National Council of the Churches of Christ in the USA. Used by permission. All rights reserved.

British Library Cataloguing-in-Publication Data
A catalogue record for this book is available from the British Library

ISBN 978–0–281–06697–1
eBook ISBN 978–0–281–06698–8

Typeset by Graphicraft Limited, Hong Kong
First printed in Great Britain by Ashford Colour Press
Subsequently digitally printed in Great Britain

eBook by Graphicraft Limited, Hong Kong

Produced on paper from sustainable forests

Contents

List of contributors vii
Foreword ix
Introduction xi
Editor's note xii

1 BAHA'I

Naw-Ruz: Beginning of spring (21 March) 2
Emma Burford

Ridvan: Baha' Ullah's time in the Garden of Ridvan
(sunset 21 April to sunset 2 May) 8
Emma Burford

The ascension of Baha' Ullah (29 May) 13
Jenny Tuxford

The martyrdom of the Bab (9 July) 16
Jenny Tuxford

2 BUDDHISM

Bodhi Day: The enlightenment of Buddha (8 December) 20
Jude Scrutton

Magha Puja: Fourfold Assembly day
(usually February/March – movable festival) 24
Jude Scrutton

Wesak: Birth, enlightenment and death of Buddha
(April/May – movable festival) 27
Jude Scrutton

3 CHRISTIANITY

St Francis (4 October) 32
Laurence Chilcott

Epiphany: The coming of the wise men (6 January) 35
Rebecca Parkinson

Candlemas: Jesus' presentation at the temple ceremony remembered
(2 February or nearest Sunday) 38
John Challis

Corpus Christi: The body of Christ
(Thursday after Trinity Sunday – movable festival) 41
Laurence Chilcott

Lent: Jesus fasting in the desert (spring – movable festival) 44
Rebecca Parkinson

Ascension – Jesus says goodbye to his friends and ascends into heaven
(Thursday, 40 days after Easter – movable festival) 47
Laurence Chilcott

Pentecost: Beginning of the Christian Church
(Sunday, 50 days after Easter – movable festival) 50
Laurence Chilcott

Ignatius of Loyola (31 July) 54
Rebecca Parkinson

4 HINDUISM

Diwali: Festival of lights
(October/November – movable festival) 58
Alan M. Barker

Ganesh Chaturthi: Birthday of the elephant-headed god
(August/September – movable festival) 61
Alan M. Barker

Holi: Festival of colour (February/March, movable festival) 64
Alan M. Barker

Janmashtami: Birth of Krishna
(August/September – movable festival) 67
Alan M. Barker

Raksha Bandhan: A festival for brothers and sisters
(usually August – movable festival) 70
Alan M. Barker

Vasant Panchami: A new beginning
(January/February – movable festival) 73
Alan M. Barker

5 ISLAM

Al-Hijra: Muhammad's migration from Mecca to Medina, Islamic New Year
(varies – movable festival) 76
Janice Ross

Eid ul-Adha: Festival of sacrifice (varies – movable festival) 80
Jude Scrutton

Eid ul-Fitr: End of Ramadan (varies – movable festival) 82
Janice Ross

Ramadan: Month-long fast (varies – movable festival) 86
Janice Ross

6 JAINISM

Mahavira Jayanti: Mahavira's birthday (March/April – movable festival) 90
Rebecca Parkinson

Paryusana: A time to pray and learn
(August/September – movable festival) 94
Rebecca Parkinson

7 JUDAISM

Rosh Hashanah: Jewish New Year, Day of Remembrance, Day of Judgement
(September/October – movable festival) 98
Manon Ceridwen Parry

Yom Kippur: Day of Atonement
(September/October – movable festival) 101
Manon Ceridwen Parry

Sukkot: Feast of Tabernacles and Harvest
(September/October – movable festival) 104
Manon Ceridwen Parry

Hanukkah: Festival of Lights (December – movable festival) 108
Manon Ceridwen Parry

Tu bi-Sebat: New Year of Trees (January/February – movable festival) 111
Emma Burford

8 SIKHISM

Birthday of Guru Nanak: Celebration to remember teaching of equality
(October/November – movable festival) 122
Helen Redfern

Hola Mohalla: Celebration of valour and defence preparedness
(March – movable festival) 125
Helen Redfern

Baisakhi: Sikh New Year and celebration of commitment (13 April) 129
Helen Redfern

Martyrdom of Guru Arjan: The consequences of jealousy (16 June) 133
Helen Redfern

9 ZOROASTRIANISM

No Ruz: Zoroastrian New Year (21 March – movable festival) 138
Gordon Lamont

Zartusht-no-diso: Remembering the first Zoroastrian prophet
(26 May/26 December – movable festival) 141
Gordon Lamont

Index 145

Contributors

Alan M. Barker is a Methodist minister who has worked in Lincolnshire for the past 25 years. Currently serving in South Holland, he helps to lead assemblies/collective worship in six local schools. A longstanding, popular contributor to SPCK's assemblies website at <www.assemblies.org.uk>, Alan also enjoys photography and the countryside.

Emma Burford trained as an actor at Rose Bruford College and then as a drama teacher at the Central School of Speech and Drama. She spent two years as a professional actor and now teaches drama at a secondary school in Putney. Emma writes assemblies and full-length plays for children of all ages and is resident playwright at the Shine Youth Theatre in south-west London.

John Challis trained as a photographer and was general manager of a photographic retail company in the early 1990s. He later studied for ordination at St Stephen's House, Oxford, and has served the Church of England as a deacon and priest in Crawley, West Sussex, Buxted and Hadlow Down, East Sussex, and Upper Beeding with Bramber and Botolphs, West Sussex. He has been a school governor for over ten years in four schools and has three children, two dogs, one cat, twelve chickens and a long-suffering but very supportive wife, Jenny.

Laurence Chilcott lives in Porthcawl, Wales. He spent 38 years in the teaching profession, 12 as a headteacher at a school in Bridgend. Now retired, he volunteers at a local school, is an active Rotarian, sings in a mixed choir and is the secretary of a Baptist church. Any spare time is taken up with walking, gardening and entertaining his grandchildren. He enjoys sharing some of the many assemblies he gave over the years on SPCK's assemblies website at <www.assemblies.org.uk> and hopes to continue to do so in the future.

Gordon Lamont is a freelance writer, radio producer and consultant. Much of his work is with the highly respected BBC Learning Division. Gordon is an agnostic who values assemblies as times of celebration and reflection on both personal growth and the big issues of life. He is the founding editor of <www.assemblies.org.uk>.

Ronni Lamont is a freelance writer and trainer who specializes in children's spirituality. Previously a teacher of science and dance at a secondary school, she then enjoyed 16 years in parish ministry as an Anglican priest. The editor of SPCK's assemblies website at <www.assemblies.org.uk>, she now writes far fewer assemblies than she did previously!

Rebecca Parkinson lives in Lancashire with her husband Ted and their two children. Since graduating from Nottingham and Manchester Universities, Rebecca has worked as a teacher, science teacher adviser and university lecturer. She writes regularly for SPCK's assemblies website at <www.assemblies.org.uk> and is the author of a number of children's books. Along with her husband, Rebecca also leads the youth and children's work at a local church. In her spare time she enjoys any type of sport, especially netball, badminton, kayaking and other outdoor pursuits.

Manon Ceridwen Parry is the rector of Llanddulas and Llysfaen, near Colwyn Bay, and also Director of Exploring Faith for St Asaph Diocese. Throughout her ministry she has taken assemblies in a variety of church and community primary schools, in both English and Welsh. She also writes poetry and has had several poems published in literary magazines and journals.

Helen Redfern loves writing assemblies and stories that communicate, inspire, stimulate and challenge. Having five children of her own keeps her in touch with popular culture and the big issues currently engaging children's interest. She has enjoyed delivering her assemblies at her local primary school.

Janice Ross lives with her husband Angus and miniature schnauzer Skara in the beautiful islands of Orkney. She loves pottering about on the beaches, collecting shells and driftwood, especially when her three granddaughters come to visit. Janice writes educational resources for Christian schools and homeschooling parents.

Jude Scrutton was born in Northamptonshire but moved to the north-west of England for his university years, where he studied PE and teaching at Edge Hill University College. He is a teacher and spent two years teaching in Singapore. Married with two wonderful children, Emily and Asher, Jude enjoys playing all sports, particularly hockey and football, and is an avid Manchester United fan.

Jenny Tuxford is a retired junior school teacher. In her spare time she likes to paint in watercolours and write stories for children. She has had three books published and is working on the next – *Fred Boggitt and the Isle of Wight Adventure*.

Foreword

It has been said that school assemblies used to be an opportunity to give the school a hymn, a prayer and a ticking off. Fortunately, those days are mostly in the past and much effort is put into making assemblies engaging and stimulating.

Teachers, however, are not well served by the confusion that often surrounds these events. Are they times of collective worship or are they assemblies and what's the difference? How Christian do they have to be or, indeed, how religious? Is compulsory worship a contradiction in terms? If we get it wrong, will we be chased by parents, governors, the National Secular Society, the Secretary of State, the Archbishop of Canterbury – or is nobody bothered?

The situation is even more complex when multifaith issues are so difficult for a secularized society to understand. We know that the 1988 Education Act requires a daily act of worship to be 'wholly or mainly of a Christian character', but there is a tendency for everyone to do what is right in their own eyes.

As ever, the most reliable way for teachers to get through some of these conundrums is to look for quality resources in the context of good practice, which is where this book comes to the rescue. It's only a start, but here are assemblies that understand the complexities and speak confidently of what can be done.

The assemblies offered here understand and respect the different faith traditions and go beyond the 'food and festivals' approach into which some have lapsed. They seek to enter the experiences they describe and so honour the inner life of the faiths and the core meanings of the festivals.

Whether or not these assemblies will work in your school is an unknown, but you try them! The experienced practitioners who have prepared them, under the watchful eye of editor Ronni Lamont, offer these assemblies for you to use as written or adapt for your own context. I'm sure that they will be of real help, both in their content and the style with which they are given shape.

More please!

John Pritchard
Bishop of Oxford
Chair, Church of England Board of Education

Introduction

Welcome to this collection of almost all new assemblies that celebrate the multifaith nature of our world. The book is designed to help teachers celebrate with all their pupils as they go through the year, no matter which faith they belong to.

As you will see from the Contents page, many festivals are 'movable' as they are dependent on the stage reached in a lunar or other calendar, so do check the dates for the current year using one of the calendars available online.

This is an exciting work for us at <www.assemblies.org.uk>. We hope that you will use the book to make your worship as inclusive as possible, as well as a resource for your RE departments. By increasing our knowledge of the different faiths, we can grow together into more accepting and inclusive communities, and your school community will be able to share what they have experienced with families and friends outside school.

All the assemblies have been written by people with a Christian background, so they conform with the present law concerning collective worship in schools.

Enjoy!

Ronni Lamont
Editor
www.assemblies.org.uk

Editor's note

The assemblies in this book are grouped into parts, each focusing on a particular religion, and these parts cover the religions in alphabetical order. Assemblies covering the religious festivals of the Baha'i faith, Buddhism, Christianity, Judaism, Sikhism and Zoroastrianism appear in their respective parts in date order, according to the British school year. The dates for the religious festivals of Hinduism, Islam and Jainism can vary widely, so the assemblies dedicated to the religious festivals of these faiths are arranged alphabetically in their respective parts.

In order to ascertain the date of a religious festival for any given year, visit:

<www.bbc.co.uk/religion/tools/calendar>

<www.reonline.org.uk/festivals/>.

1
BAHA'I

NAW-RUZ
Beginning of spring (21 March)

By Emma Burford

Suitable for Key Stage 2 (script suitable for Years 3 to 6)

Aims

To explain the Baha'i faith holy day of Naw-Ruz through performance and encourage understanding of different religious holy days.

Preparation and materials

- **Background** The Baha'i faith is the youngest of the world's religions. It grew out of the Babi faith or sect – a Shi'ite branch of Islam – founded by Mirza 'Ali Muhammad in Iran in 1844. He became known as the Bab. Later, Mirza Hoseyn 'Ali Nuri, a fervent disciple of the Bab, adopted the name Baha' Ullah, and their followers regarded them as the most recent of God's messengers, others being Abraham, Moses, Buddha, Zoroaster, Christ and Muhammad. The Baha'i faith came into being in 1863 when Baha' Ullah declared himself to be the messenger of God foretold by the Bab. It is centred on the idea that all people belong to one human family and the time has come to recognize this and work for the unity of all people.
- **Staging ideas** Split the stage into three sections: the left side is an area for Miss Cook, Mr Green and the Principles; the centre is for the family; the right side is for the presenter and Professor Kew. In the centre, the four children could sit on the floor or around a table. The scene could be set in a kitchen, living room or outside.
- **Costume ideas** I always find the best costumes are the simple ones that symbolize a character – for example, all the children in black clothes with pieces showing certain characters in colours, such as Gran wearing a light blue woollen cardigan and the Principles each wearing a colourful sash saying what their principle is. Ask the children – they will be sure to have lots of ideas!

- **Links with art** The children could create posters that explain the equinox and hold them up during Professor Kew's explanation. You could also produce pictures and posters to accompany the three core principles of the Baha'i faith.

Pronunciation notes:

Naw-Ruz	gnaw-ruz
Baha'i	ba-high
Baha' Ullah	bah-hah oo-la

Assembly

1. Say, 'Today we are going to introduce you to a festival that is happening this month to celebrate spring. Let's watch the children tell their story.'

2. The children give their performance, following the script below. You will need children to be the following members of the cast:

Mum	Miss Cook
Dad	Presenter
Gran	Professor Kew
Child 1	Mr Khan
Child 2	Principle 1
Child 3	Principle 2
Child 4	Principle 3
Big Brother	
Big Sister	

Mum: That's it! I've finally put away all your Christmas presents! It's only taken me three months!

Dad: Why is it that at Christmas the living room always looks like one giant toy shop?

Gran: So many presents! I remember, we never had that many when I was a girl.

Child 1: We know Gran, we are very lucky!

Mum: Anyway, at least this means I can now get on with my spring cleaning.

Child 1: Ah! Mum's legendary spring clean!

Child 2: Spring has definitely arrived, then!

Child 3: Well, it should do anyway . . . because it's the holy day of Naw-Ruz.

Gran: Naw-Ruz? What is this Naw-Ruz?

Mum: I can't say I've heard of it either!

Dad: Is it a new computer game or something?

Child 4: No, Dad, it marks the coming of spring.

Child 3: Oh, I remember that from last year! Miss Cook said.

Miss Cook: Naw-Ruz is one of the nine holy days of the Baha'i faith.

Child 3: She said.

Miss Cook: It always falls on or around the twenty-first of March.

Child 1: Which is the vernal equinox, apparently.

Dad: The vernal equinox?

Big Brother: Hi everyone, what are we talking about?

Dad: The vernal equinox.

Big Brother: Oh . . . what's that?

Child 2: Well, the word 'vernal' comes from the Latin word 'ver', meaning spring.

Dad: When did you get so clever?!

Child 1: We learnt it from a video we watched.

Presenter: Hello and welcome to 'Science Explained'. Today we are talking about the wonderful world of the equinox, and here to explain it is Professor Charlie Kew.

Professor Kew: An equinox happens twice a year each year and marks the moment when the location on the Earth's equator known as the subsolar point is vertically below the centre of the sun. This normally happens around the twentieth or twenty-first of March and twenty-second or twenty-third of September each year.

Child 2: So that's how we get the date for Naw-Ruz – it's at the beginning of spring.

Child 1: It's the beginning of spring cleaning in our house.

Big Brother: OK, I think I get it, but who celebrates this holy day?

Child 4: I thought you were cleverer than us!

Big Brother: Not in everything, I admit. We never learnt this when I was at school.

Big Sister: What are we all doing? Everyone seems to be listening very carefully!

Dad: We're learning about Naw-Ruz.

Mum: The holy day for the coming of spring.

Gran: It's on the same day as the vernal equinox.

Big Sister: That being . . . ?

Gran: It's the coming of spring, when the sun is directly above a point on the equator.

Child 4: Wow, Gran. Well remembered!

Child 3: You're all taking it in!

Child 2: We're teaching our parents!

Big Brother: You were just about to tell us: which religion celebrates this holy day?

Child 1: Oh, that's easy! It's celebrated in the Baha'i faith.

Child 2: It developed out of Babism.

Child 4: Miss Cook said . . .

Miss Cook: The Baha'i faith started in the nineteenth century in Persia. The Baha'i faith has three core principles. They will tell us what they are.

Principle 1: I am the first principle and I teach the unity of God.

Principle 2: I am the second principle and I teach the unity of religion.

Principle 3: I am the third principle and I teach the unity of humankind.

Miss Cook: Thank you, principles. In the Baha'i faith, then, the main aim is world peace.

Mum: I must tell Miss Cook what a wonderful teacher she is.

Dad: I know, the children are remembering all this information she taught them!

Child 3: It's celebrated in countries such as Iran, where it's a national holiday, and India, Pakistan, Turkey . . .

Child 4: Azerbaijan.

Child 1: Afghanistan.

Child 2: Tajikistan.

Dad: So it's from the Baha'i faith . . . ?

Child 2: Yep. Baha' Ullah was the founder of the faith.

Child 3: He was the founder and made Naw-Ruz a holy day.

Big Sister: He said that Naw-Ruz means the beginning of spring?

Child 4: Well, we had an assembly on him and his son 'Abd ol-Baha.

Child 1: Baha' Ullah's successor.

Child 3: Mr Khan told us . . .

Mr Khan: Baha' Ullah said that Naw-Ruz was associated with the Most Great Name of God and was a festival for those who had observed the fast.

Big Brother: *(To big sister)* That's when . . .

Big Sister: I know! When you don't eat any food.

Big Brother: That would be difficult for you!

Big Sister: Shall we move on!

Mr Khan: 'Abd ol-Baha, Baha' Ullah's son, explained that Naw-Ruz is to celebrate the spiritual springtime and the bringing of new life.

Mum: It really does sound like a lovely festival.

Gran: What do they do at this festival?

Child 1: There's prayer, music and dancing.

Child 2: And, as those who observe the holy festival have been fasting, a huge dinner.

Dad: Sounds good to me!

Mum: Well, I'm very glad that you have learnt something about this festival.

Dad: Me too. You kids are turning out all right!

Mum: You'll be even better when you all help me celebrate the coming of spring with some feather dusters, a vacuum cleaner and some elbow grease.

Children: Oh, Mum!

Child 2: I think I definitely prefer the way Naw-Ruz celebrates springtime.

Time for reflection

Spend some time thinking about the joy and the wonder of spring, of new life.

Prayer
Help us to learn about all other religious ceremonies, festivals and celebrations so we can appreciate all the wonders of your world.
Amen

 Song

'Think of a world without any flowers' (*Come and Praise*, 17)

RIDVAN
Baha' Ullah's time in the Garden of Ridvan (sunset 21 April to sunset 2 May)

By Emma Burford

Suitable for Key Stage 2 (script suitable for Years 3 to 6)

Aims

To explain the Baha'i faith holy day of Ridvan through performance and encourage understanding of different religious holy days.

Preparation and materials

- **Background** The Baha'i faith is the youngest of the world's religions. It grew out of the Babi faith or sect – a Shi'ite branch of Islam – founded by Mirza 'Ali Muhammad in Iran in 1844. He became known as the Bab. Later, Mirza Hoseyn 'Ali Nuri, a fervent disciple of the Bab, adopted the name Baha' Ullah, and their followers regarded them as the most recent of God's messengers, others being Abraham, Moses, Buddha, Zoroaster, Christ and Muhammad. The Baha'i faith came into being in 1863 when Baha' Ullah declared himself to be the messenger of God foretold by the Bab. It is centred on the idea that all people belong to one human family and the time has come to recognize this and work for the unity of all people. The festival of Ridvan (pronounced riz-wan) is significant because it celebrates the time when Baha' Ullah officially announced that he was the prophet proclaimed by the Bab. The festival takes its name from the garden on the outskirts of Baghdad in which this happened. It became known as the Garden of Ridvan (paradise).
- **Staging ideas** There are several ways you could stage this performance. You could have the four gardens sitting on four stage blocks spread across the stage. The children could then stand up when reading their letters – the extra characters then standing around the stage block when saying their lines. Another way would be to have one stage block and each garden would

then step up on to it when saying their lines. You could then have all the other action taking place around the one stage block. For this script there are only 12 characters. In order to include more children in the performance, miming could be added to the speeches – for example, when a garden is talking about how the word has got around about it, the children could mime a message being passed around the stage (Chinese whispers-style) and they could create the river that the family crosses with a long piece of blue material.
- **Costumes ideas** I always find the best costumes are the simple ones that symbolize a character – for example, all the children in black with the gardens wearing green tunics and the festivals wearing colourful tunics. Ask the children – they will be sure to have lots of ideas!
- **Links with art** If there is a certain flair for art in the class, the children could create more elaborate garden costumes – leaves could be created with hand prints, for example.

Pronunciation notes:

Baha'i	ba-high
Baha' Ullah	bah-hah oo-la
Najibiyyih	najeeb-buy-ee
Ridvan	riz-wan

Assembly

1. Say, 'Today we are going to introduce you to a story that takes place in Baghdad. The story uses letters that the Garden of Najibiyyih sent to a friend explaining how the garden eventually became the Garden of Ridvan. Let's watch and listen to how the letters tell the story.

2. The children give their performance, following the script below. You will need children to be the following members of the cast:

Garden 1	Festival 1
Garden 2	Festival 2
Garden 3	Festival 3
Garden 4	Festival 4
Gardener	Festival 5
Muhammad-Najib Pasha	
Baha' Ullah	

Garden 1: Twenty-first of April 1863

My dear new friend,

This is the first letter to you. As we have just met, let me introduce myself. I am the Najibiyyih Garden.

Gardener: The garden is to the north of the city of Baghdad and to the east of the Tigris River. It is wooded with a wall all the way round and four paths, lined with roses, leading to a circular area in the middle.

Garden 1: I was created for the governor of Baghdad – Muhammad-Najib Pasha.

Muhammad-Najib Pasha: I was the governor of Baghdad from 1842 until 1847. I had the garden built with my palace situated at the edge. The garden was named after me.

Garden 1: Can you believe that I was created with a palace? I am a beautiful garden. People are in awe of me. I know that I am destined for great things.

Your friend,
Najibiyyih Garden

Garden 2: Twenty-second of April 1863

My dear friend,

There has been someone new to visit me. His name is Baha' Ullah and he is the founder of the Baha'i faith. I have heard that he has been banished to Baghdad by the government because of his influence over the citizens in Tehran. He travelled across the Tigris River with some of his family. Once he arrived here, he made an announcement that I overheard.

Baha' Ullah: For the next eleven days I will receive visitors before I travel to Constantinople.

Garden 2: I will watch him work, my friend, and tell you all about it. I know the people of Baghdad will be sorrowful to see Baha' Ullah leave them. I do not know this man, but will get to know him as he stays in my garden.

I will write again soon, friend,
Najibiyyih Garden

Garden 3: Second of May, 1863

My dear friend,

I have so much to tell you. The past eleven days have been so wonderful and enlightening. I have observed Baha' Ullah meet with government officials and all sorts of people. The rest of Baha' Ullah's family have finally arrived on the ninth day – the Tigris River had risen so much that they were unable to cross it. Baha' Ullah and his family have now made their way to Constantinople, but before he left, my friend Baha' Ullah gave me the new name of Ridvan, meaning 'paradise'. I can't believe it! I told you before, my friend, I am destined for great things.

Your friend,
The Garden of Ridvan

Garden 4: Third of May, 1863

My dear friend,

This will be my last letter to you. I had to tell you about a festival that is now named after me! Many people have told me about the festival of Ridvan.

Festival 1: Ridvan is a twelve-day festival.

Garden 4: That is because this was how long Baha' Ullah stayed in my garden.

Festival 2: It is one of the two 'Most Great Festivals' and is celebrated by the Baha'is between the twenty-first of April and the second of May.

Festival 3: The first, ninth and twelfth days are holy days.

Garden 4: The first is to celebrate Baha' Ullah arriving at my garden, the ninth is when Baha' Ullah's family arrived and the twelfth is when Baha' Ullah left for Constantinople – now called Istanbul.

Festival 4: During these three days work is prohibited.

Festival 5: On those three days, too, people come together in prayer, followed by celebrations.

Garden 4: So, friend, thanks to Baha' Ullah, I will always be known and celebrated for centuries to come.

Your friend,
The Garden of Ridvan

Time for reflection

Spend a few moments thinking about how religions and figures of the past have struggled to be heard. We are thankful that there are so many religions in the world, helping us to think about God and making our world a more interesting place.

 Song

'Morning has broken' (*Come and Praise*, 1)

THE ASCENSION OF BAHA' ULLAH (29 May)

By Jenny Tuxford

Suitable for Key Stage 2

Aims

To understand the basic beliefs of the Baha'i faith by considering the life and death of Baha' Ullah and thinking about our own behaviour and attitudes towards others.

Preparation and materials

- **Background** The Baha'i faith is the youngest of the world's religions. It grew out of the Babi faith or sect – a Shi'ite branch of Islam – founded by Mirza 'Ali Muhammad in Iran in 1844. He became known as the Bab. Later, Mirza Hoseyn 'Ali Nuri, a fervent disciple of the Bab, adopted the name Baha' Ullah, and their followers regarded them as the most recent of God's messengers, others being Abraham, Moses, Buddha, Zoroaster, Christ and Muhammad. The Baha'i faith came into being in 1863 when Baha' Ullah declared himself to be the messenger of God foretold by the Bab. It is centred on the idea that all people belong to one human family and the time has come to recognize this and work for the unity of all people.

Pronunciation notes:

Baha'i	ba-high
Baha' Ullah	bah-hah oo-la
Mirza Hoseyn 'Ali Nuri	meer-sah hoosayn al-ee noo-ri
Baha	bah-hah
Bahji	bar-ji

Assembly

1. Explain to the children that the Baha'i faith originated in a country called Persia – now called Iran. Show them where it is on a map. The Baha'i faith is one of the world's youngest religions, yet it has around seven million followers.

2. Explain that Baha'is see everyone in the world as one big family. They strongly believe in the idea of 'virtues' and the notion that people should live a virtuous life. 'Virtuous' means a person being good – by having kind thoughts and showing kindness in many different ways.

3. Give the children some examples of virtues – such as love, honesty, generosity, kindness, truthfulness, consideration. See if they can come up with others. Another way to express this might be in the form of phrases – for example, not call people names, be kind to someone lonely, do as your parents ask, try hard with homework and so on.

4. Like flowers, virtues bring joy and beauty to the world. There are some lovely ways to present these ideas to the children. You could draw candles and put pictures of the children on the candles. Every time the children demonstrate virtues, draw beams of light emanating from the candles and write the virtues on them. Baha'is encourage children to talk about the virtues they have demonstrated. Here is one example: 'I got full marks for my homework – a poem that I wrote. Everybody loved it. My sister helped me. When others praised me, I told them that my sister helped me.' This shows the virtues of honesty, humility and justice.

5. Tell the children the following story.

   ### How the Baha'i faith began
   In 1817, a man called Mirza Hoseyn 'Ali Nuri was born in Persia. His family was rich and he lived the life of a prince. He was very clever and wise, his knowledge of religions exceptional, even though he had not studied them. From an early age, he knew that his mission was to spread a message of peace and unity and the idea that everyone should work together for the good of humanity. This undertaking meant that he would say 'Goodbye' to all his worldly wealth, for the authorities stripped him of his wealth and property and banished him to Baghdad.

   Mirza Hoseyn 'Ali Nuri changed his name to Baha' Ullah – Baha for short. The name Baha' Ullah means 'the Glory of God'. Baha spent his life helping others. His work for charity earned him the nickname 'Father of the Poor'.

   Was everybody happy to listen to his ideas? No, they were not. That is because Baha's beliefs were not the same as those of the Muslims who lived in Baghdad at that time. They thought that far too many people were listening to him – people from many towns and cities were drawn to him by his wisdom and holiness.

For his efforts to try and help his fellow human beings, Baha was thrown into prison more than once. He was tortured and narrowly escaped a death sentence when someone made up lies about him, saying that he had tried to kill the ruler of Persia. Even his own brother tried to kill him with poison.

While he was chained up in a terrible prison known as the 'Black Pit', he was surrounded by the worst criminals you can imagine, but it was here that he had two visions – sent by God, he believed – telling him that he was the 'Promised One'. Here, also, he wrote 100 books.

Baha' Ullah died peacefully on 29 May 1892, aged 75. He was still a prisoner then, but had been allowed to live outside the walls. Love and laughter were two of his great gifts.

6. Every year, on 29 May, at 3 a.m. (4 a.m. in the UK), Baha'is celebrate the ascension of Baha' Ullah, when this remarkable man's soul ascended to meet his God. He is buried in Bahji, in Israel, in a shrine surrounded by a stunning garden.

Time for reflection

Spend a little while remembering how Baha suffered because of what he believed to be the right way to live – in peace and kindness. How could we copy that example today?

Prayer
Please help us all to be as kind and loving as we can be, living with others in unity, a strong worldwide community.
Amen

Baha'i prayer
We are plants of thine orchard;
the flowers of the meadow;
roses of thy garden.
Let thy rain fall upon us;
let the sun of reality shine upon us.
Thou art the giver.

Song

'I've got peace like a river' (*Come and Praise*, 143)

THE MARTYRDOM OF THE BAB (9 July)

By Jenny Tuxford

Suitable for Key Stage 2

Aim

To learn more about faith in the context of the Baha'i religion, with particular reference to the life and death of the Bab.

Preparation and materials

- **Background** The Baha'i faith is the youngest of the world's religions. It grew out of the Babi faith or sect – a Shi'ite branch of Islam – founded by Mirza 'Ali Muhammad in Iran in 1844. He became known as the Bab. Later, Mirza Hoseyn 'Ali Nuri, a fervent disciple of the Bab, adopted the name Baha' Ullah, and their followers regarded them as the most recent of God's messengers, others being Abraham, Moses, Buddha, Zoroaster, Christ and Muhammad. The Baha'i faith came into being in 1863 when Baha' Ullah declared himself to be the messenger of God foretold by the Bab. It is centred on the idea that all people belong to one human family and the time has come to recognize this and work for the unity of all people.

Pronunciation notes:

    Baha'i   ba-high

Assembly

1. Explain to the children that the Baha'i faith originated in a country called Persia – now called Iran. Show them where it is on a map. Explain, too, that many of the people in Persia follow the Islamic faith, and they are called Muslims. Muslims believe that the prophet Muhammad was the last prophet.

2. Explain to the children that you are going to tell them something about a very unusual and charismatic man who dedicated his life to God and helping people live better lives.

3. Tell them the following story.

   The martyrdom of the Bab
   In Persia, many years ago, there lived a young man called Mirza 'Ali Muhammad. He was actually descended from the great prophet Muhammad himself. He was a merchant's son and, because of his faith, he assumed the title of the Bab, which means the 'Gate' in Arabic, 'Gateway' in Persian. He believed that the way people lived their lives should be based on love and compassion. His sole ambition was to improve the world.

   The Bab had an amazing personality and he was a wonderful speaker. It is said that 'Mountains and valleys re-echoed the majesty of his voice'. People flocked in their thousands to hear him and listen to his highly unusual message. There wasn't much love and peace around in Persia at that time!

   What's more, the Bab didn't just speak to the people all the time – he was able to answer their really tricky questions.

   Even more astonishing still was that the Bab was telling them that someone even more amazing was on his way. This was wonderful news. Someone was coming who was far greater than himself and this person would bring about the start of an age of peace and justice. Brilliant! They needed some peace and justice. 'As soon as this promised teacher arrives – recognize and follow him,' the Bab told them.

   Was everybody happy about the Bab telling them that a great prophet was on his way? No way! Remember that the Muslims believed that Muhammad was the last great messenger of God? Well then, there could be no other. The Muslims weren't just unhappy, they were furious – so much so that they threw the Bab into prison. He was having far too much influence on the Persians. He even had disciples who were going about the country spreading his teachings.

   Sadly, the Bab's disciples were tortured and killed for what they were preaching. Then, after just six years of spreading his beliefs, the Bab himself was sentenced to death.

   In 1850 he was led through crowded streets to a place where he was to be executed, by firing squad, in front of 10,000 people. To everyone's horror, one of the Bab's young followers begged to be killed with him and the two men were tied up with ropes. An Armenian firing squad fired at them, but everyone was shocked and surprised when, after the smoke had cleared, they discovered that the young man was unharmed and the Bab had disappeared! Only the ropes had been damaged – they were shredded. A search party went to work and, eventually, the Bab was found – back in his cell.

After this miracle, not surprisingly, the firing squad flatly refused to try again and so a new team had to be summoned. This time they succeeded, but, amazingly, neither of the victims' faces had been wounded at all.

The bodies were unceremoniously thrown into a moat outside the city. Later, however, the Bab's followers rescued them and they were buried on Mount Carmel in Israel in a shrine that is now a place of pilgrimage for Baha'is.

4. On 9 July every year, at noon, Baha'is remember the events surrounding the death of the Bab. It is a day of rest when prayers are said. The Bab and his followers showed great courage.

Time for reflection

Spend a few moments thinking about what is important to you and be thankful for living in an inclusive and tolerant community.

Baha'i prayer
Oh Lord my God,
guide me, protect me,
illumine the lamp of my heart.
Guide me, protect me,
make me a brilliant star.

Song

'The family of man' (*Come and Praise*, 69)

2
BUDDHISM

Editor's note

Although meditation is very much associated with Buddhism, most of the major world faiths have practised and still practise it. In Christianity, for example, many of the saints meditated, especially those of the 'Desert tradition', such as Anthony of Egypt.

Current psychological research indicates the positive effects of teaching children the value of silence, so we have included opportunities to practise meditation within these assemblies. You may, of course, say prayers instead.

BODHI DAY
The enlightenment of Buddha
(8 December)

By Jude Scrutton

Suitable for whole school

Aims

To know and understand the importance of key events in religious calendars, understand the need of humanity to search for answers to life's mysteries, and learn about how Buddha gained enlightenment.

Preparation and materials

- **Background** The dates and celebration of Buddhist festivals vary greatly and not all Buddhists will celebrate the same festivals. Bodhi day is celebrated by Pure Land Buddhists, who are mainly found in Japan and the United States. Buddhism is practised all around the world, but is particularly prevalent in Sri Lanka, Burma, Thailand, Tibet, China and South Korea.
- **Props** A display of a bo (or bodh) tree, *Ficus religiosa* or holy fig, if possible, or a picture of one (visit <www.buddhanet.net>), plus other copyright-free pictures available on the internet. A candle and means to light it. Also, see if there are any Buddhist children in your school who would be willing to talk about this festival.
- **Music** 'I see the light' from the soundtrack for the Disney animated film *Tangled* (Disney, 2011), based on the story of Rapunzel (widely available online) or other music of your choice.

Pronunciation notes (local pronunciations may vary):

Bodhi	boe-dee
Siddhartha Gautama	sid-hearta go-taa-ma
King Shuddhodana	suud-hod-aana
Shakya	shack-ya
Maha Maya	ma-ha my-ya
Asita	a-see-ta

Mahaprajapati	ma-ha-pra-jap-tee
Yasodhara	ya-sho-duh-rah
Rahula	ra-hoo-la
Bodh Gaya	bo guy-ya

Assembly

1. The children enter the room to the 'I see the light' music from the soundtrack to the Disney animated film *Tangled* or music of your choice. Choose a child to sit under the tree or by the tree picture.

2. Ask the children to think about everything they know – the Earth is a sphere, there are 24 hours in a day and so on. Talk about how valuable knowledge is and, in some countries, it is suppressed by governments that fear uprisings.

3. Explain that Bodhi Day is a Buddhist festival celebrating Siddhartha Gautama's enlightenment under a Bodh tree. Explain that Bodhi Day is an important day for many Buddhists. 'Buddha' means 'enlightened one' or one who has a special understanding of things, someone who knows what is important.

4. Ask the children if they know of Prince Siddhartha's (the Buddha's) story. You could simply read out the text below, paraphrase or else make a play out of it.

How the Buddhist faith began

Buddhism began around 2,500 years ago. The foundation of Buddhism rests on the life of one teacher – an Indian prince named Siddhartha Gautama. Prince Siddhartha grew up in a small kingdom in north-east India, an area that is now in Nepal. His father, King Shuddhodana, ruled over the Shakya people. Although the king hoped his son would carry on his legacy, the prince had a very different calling – one that made him one of history's most famous and influential figures.

Prince Siddhartha was born somewhere between 566 BC and 490 BC (historians still debate the exact date), the son of King Shuddhodana and Queen Maha Maya. Before he was born, the queen felt that he was going to be a significant person in the world. Siddhartha was born in a garden and Buddhists tell of how great peace fell on the whole kingdom at that time. Siddhartha means 'the one who brings all good'. News of the

BODHI DAY 21

prince's birth spread and many visitors came to pay tribute to the baby. One of these visitors was the holy sage Asita.

Asita told the king and queen that the prince would be either a great king or a great saint. Both the king and queen were happy, but Shuddhodana wanted to be certain that his son became a great emperor, not a saint, so for years he gave Siddhartha all he could desire and ensured that he was shielded from pain and suffering as he thought that these issues would set him thinking about religion.

Tragically, Queen Maha Maya became seriously ill and, seven days after giving birth, she died. Mahaprajapati, the queen's sister, brought up Siddhartha as though he were her own son, and the prince lived a carefree childhood within the palace walls. King Shuddhodana made certain that he had the finest education, and the prince learned quickly. In fact, legend has it that, after only a few lessons, he had no need of teachers for he had learnt all they could teach him. As Siddhartha grew, his intelligence was matched by his compassionate gentleness. Unlike his friends and family, he spent a great deal of time alone, wandering the palace gardens. He did not join in with the games of other boys, but sought the company of animals and nature.

Later, he married Princess Yasodhara and they lived quietly until after the birth of a son, Rahula. Siddhartha decided to go beyond the royal enclosure and see the rest of the world. As he travelled, he met lots of people, including a holy man, meditating under a tree.

Siddhartha returned to the palace and decided that he was being called to spend time meditating, so he joined a group of hermits in the forest. He was 29 when he joined the group and he spent six years fasting, relying only on charity and studying and meditating. Despite all this work, he didn't get where he wanted to be – he didn't understand the way that the world was or how people might work to make it better.

When a young woman offered him rice milk, he took it, then sat under a bo (or bodh) tree in the town of Bodh Gaya. There he sat until he achieved what Buddhists call enlightenment – that is, understanding. He was then called Buddha – the enlightened one.

The Buddha became one of the world's greatest teachers and Buddhism was born from his teaching.

5. Ask the child under the tree if he/she feels enlightened. Ask the children, 'Where do you go when you need help and support in your lives? Where do you go when you want to be quiet and think about any problems you might have?'

Time for reflection

(Light a candle and play some gentle music to help the children meditate.)

Many people of faith spend a lot of time meditating, which is when you try to empty your mind of any distractions. For the next minute, I want you to try and think of nothing. Relax, breathing gently in and out, sit very still and perhaps close your eyes and think about the candle flame or look at it.

(Pause)

How can we hear God speaking to us if there is no quiet space in which to hear it?

> *Prayer*
> May my words and actions today bring light and life to others.
> **Amen**

Song

'Father, hear the prayer we offer' (*Come and Praise*, 48)

BODHI DAY 23

MAGHA PUJA
Fourfold Assembly day (usually February/March – movable festival)

By Jude Scrutton

Suitable for whole school

Aim

To know and understand the importance of key events in religious calendars, especially with regard to Buddhism.

Preparation and materials

- Visit <www.youtube.com/watch?v=9bX6Rlb60fE&feature=related> and <www.youtube.com/watch?v=fPkeEvjnHkA&feature=related> for videos about the ceremony. Check regarding copyright issues and school policy before showing these or other videos in the assembly.
- **Props** Have ten candles to hand out and one, lit (provide means to light it), at the front of the assembly (use sand trays to ensure safety, as per your school policy). It is possible to buy or make 'drip guards' to put on candles – these catch any dripping wax before it arrives at the bottom of the candle. Also, create a large card with the following quote displayed on it so it can be read from a distance:

    > Thousands of candles can be lit from a single candle, and the life of the candle will not be shortened. Happiness never decreases by being shared.
    >
    > (Buddha)

    It might be necessary to give a certain amount of background information on Buddha and who he is, depending on the knowledge of the children in the assembly, so have this to hand if required for your group.

    Pronunciation notes (local pronunciations may vary):

Magha Puja	mag-ha poo-ja
Siddhartha	sid-hearta

Assembly

1. As the children enter the hall for the assembly, give out the candles, but keep one, lit, at the front. Once assembled, ask the children with candles to stand.
2. Ask the children, 'How can we light the candles?' Hopefully they will suggest using the flame of the lit candle to light the others.
3. Ask them to come up and light their candles from the lit one. Once completed, ask the children, 'Was the original candle affected by sharing its light?' Tell them happiness is like this, and Buddha used candles to teach this important life lesson. Show the children the large card with the quote from Buddha on it:

   > Thousands of candles can be lit from a single candle, and the life of the candle will not be shortened. Happiness never decreases by being shared.
   >
   > (Buddha)

4. Give the children background information about who Buddha was and so on, if required.
5. Explain that, soon after Prince Siddhartha had experienced enlightenment and become the first Buddha, there was an important event that took place: 1,250 monks spontaneously travelled to the Bamboo Grove temple to see Buddha. These monks were all Buddha's direct disciples and the meeting was called the Fourfold Assembly. At the Assembly, Buddha gave the following teaching:
   - not to do any evil
   - to do good
   - to purify the mind.

   Buddhists today around the world observe Magha Puja to commemorate this event.
6. Show the two videos listed under 'Preparation and materials' (or others from the internet that do not infringe copyright and that align with school policy), to show how different Buddhists observe Magha Puja.

Time for reflection

(Play some gentle music to help the children meditate.)

Many people of faith spend a lot of time meditating, which is when you try to empty your mind of any distractions. For the next minute, I want you to try and think of nothing. Relax, breathing gently in and out, sit very still and perhaps close your eyes and think about the candle flame or look at it.

(Pause)

How can we hear God speaking to us if there is no quiet space in which to hear it?

> *Prayer for peace*
> May peace come
> Peace in our school
> Peace in our community
> Peace in our country
> Peace in our world
> And may it begin with me.

Song

'In Christ there is no East or West' (*Come and Praise*, 66)

WESAK
Birth, enlightenment and death of Buddha (April/May – movable festival)

By Jude Scrutton

Suitable for whole school

Aim

To know and understand the importance of key events in religious calendars, especially with regard to Buddhism.

Preparation and materials

- **Background** Wesak (sometimes spelt Vesak) is often known informally as Buddha's birthday, but is, in fact, the day on which Buddhists celebrate the birth, enlightenment and death of their founder, Siddhartha Gautama – better known as Buddha. This annual festival is observed by Buddhists across the world, especially in many south-east Asian countries, such as Thailand, Cambodia, Sri Lanka, Malaysia, Myanmar, Singapore, Vietnam, Nepal, Indonesia, China and Taiwan, which have large numbers of practising Buddhists.

    The actual date of Wesak varies depending on which lunar calendar is used – different ones are used in different traditions – and from year to year, but generally falls in April or May.

- **Props** These are optional: a birthday cake, pretend wrapped birthday presents, a large map of the world, displayed, and a statue of Buddha, plus a small jug of water. You will also need a candle and means to light it.

Pronunciation notes (local pronunciations may vary):

Wesak	we-sak
Mawlid	more-lid
Siddhartha Gautama	sid-hearta go-taa-ma

Assembly

1. Ask the children (and staff) to put their hands up if it is their birthday today. Ask the children to share how they celebrate their birthdays. Bring in the props listed above at appropriate moments, if using.

2. Ask the children what is special about 25 December. You could also ask them if they know what Mawlid celebrates (this is the birthday of the prophet Muhammad).

3. Discuss the fact that 6 per cent of the people in the world are Buddhists. Ask the children if anyone can say where Buddhism originated? (India).

4. Explain that Buddhism is largely based on the teachings of Siddhartha Gautama, who was a prince, but left his life of luxury to embark on a long and hard journey to enlightenment. He was born somewhere between 566 BC and 490 BC (historians still debate the exact date) on a day with a full moon. The young prince was named Siddhartha, which means 'the one who brings all good'. His parents ruled a small kingdom in northern India.

5. Wesak celebrates the birth of this prince who later became Buddha, and is the most important of the Buddhist festivals for the millions of Buddhists around the world. In thousands of temples across the world, from Tokyo in the East to San Francisco in the West, Buddhists pay homage to this Indian prince who gave up the pleasures of a royal household to bring peace and happiness to humanity.

6. Today, Wesak is celebrated with lots of colour and happiness. Homes are cleaned and decorated. In many countries, during the festival, Buddhists visit their local temple for services and teaching and give offerings of food, candles and flowers to the monks. Chanting and praying are an important part of Wesak.

7. The following could be done visually: bathing the Buddha. Pour the water over the shoulders of the Buddha statue as a reminder that we need to purify our minds of greed, hatred and ignorance. In Wesak, gifts are taken to an altar to be offered to the Buddha statues. This shows respect and gratitude to the Buddha for his life and teachings.

Time for reflection

(Meditation is central to Buddhist practice, but difficult to master, so we have repeated the chance to meditate here, following on from the

previous assembly, to give the children time to practise. Light a candle and play some gentle music to help the children meditate.)

Many people of faith spend a lot of time meditating, which is when you try to empty your mind of any distractions. For the next minute, I want you to try and think of nothing. Relax, breathing gently in and out, sit very still and perhaps close your eyes and think about the candle flame or look at it.

(Pause)

How can we hear God speaking to us if there is no quiet space in which to hear it?

> *Prayer for peace*
> May peace come
> Peace in our school
> Peace in our community
> Peace in our country
> Peace in our world
> And may it begin with me.

Song

You could sing 'Happy birthday' to Siddhartha Gautama, Buddha, and any children (and members of staff) who have a birthday today.

3
CHRISTIANITY

ST FRANCIS
(4 October)

By Laurence Chilcott

Suitable for whole school

Aim

To learn about Francis and appreciate how he was thinking about our relationship with the environment long before the green movement of relatively recent years.

Preparation and materials

- **Background** Francis was born around 1182 and died at the age of 44 or 45. He founded the Franciscan Order of Friars and the Poor Clares, and his feast day is 4 October.
- **Props** Display pictures of statues of Francis, often shown with animals or birds. Alongside, display your school's 'Green Flag' or other environmental award.

Assembly

1. It is only in recent years people have begun to realize that we need to take care of our world so that people who come after us will be able to enjoy it. We have natural resources that will not last for ever and we know that we need to reduce waste and re-use or recycle what we can.

2. Scientists continue to work to develop more efficient ways of producing energy to power machines and cars, and heat our homes. The power of the wind, the sun and the waves are all examples of renewable resources – ones that can be used time and time again without running out.

3. Schools, too, have become more aware of the environment, and many have worked to gain the Green Flag or other environmental awards. Often children have helped to teach their parents how they can save energy and reduce waste.

4. Francis, who lived over 800 years ago, believed that we all have a duty to protect our world and care for all creatures that

live in it. He was thinking of conservation and sustainability long before the world realized just how important they are, so it is not surprising that he is the patron saint of animals and the environment. Let me tell you his story.

How Francis came to be a saint

In his youth, Francis didn't have much time for the environment – he was too busy enjoying himself. He came from a wealthy family and made the most of the good times that his family money could buy. He loved sport, wore the most fashionable clothes and enjoyed feasting on the best food and wine with his friends.

In his early twenties, Francis became a soldier, but things did not go well for him – he was captured and spent a year in prison. Not long after he returned home, he was taken ill and around that time began to think about what he would do with his life. He had become more and more dissatisfied with the way money had become so important to him and decided to serve God in any way he could.

Francis began by helping the sick and restoring churches that had become derelict, but he also spent a lot of time walking in lonely places, praying that God would make it clear how he could best serve him. Eventually, he realized that his wealth was holding him back from serving God, so he decided to give up all his possessions and money. Francis' father was very displeased with him and tried to persuade him that he was making the biggest mistake of his life. His friends made fun of him and thought he had gone mad, too, but Francis had made up his mind and could not be persuaded to change it.

Wearing a rough cloak and going barefoot, he walked from place to place, telling people about God's love and forgiveness. Soon others joined him in the work, and they lived in a deserted house near Francis' home town of Assisi, in Italy. He called those who joined him 'brothers' and set them one very simple rule, which was 'To follow the teachings of our Lord Jesus Christ and to walk in his footsteps'.

In those days you really needed a licence from the Pope in Rome if you wanted to preach, so Francis went with his first brothers to Rome, where he was granted one. And so the Franciscan Order, as it became known, was officially recognized. In time, it grew and grew, but the things that remained most important of all were to imitate Christ and carry out his work and not keep possessions or money for themselves. Francis believed that money and possessions would stop people from worshipping God properly because, often, it was all they thought about.

Respect for nature and animals was also very important to Francis and it is said that he had a special way with animals as they did not seem to be afraid of him. We are told that one day he even preached to the birds that surrounded him as he walked in the woods. Another story about him is that he spoke to a wolf that had been killing animals and even attacking people in a village. The wolf sat at Francis' feet and Francis warned him to stop his attacks and make peace with the people. Francis led the wolf into the village and made a pact that if the villagers fed the wolf he would never attack again – and that's just what happened.

The Franciscan Order is still going today and the monks continue to follow the rules and teaching of Francis. They often live in small groups, helping people who are in need, and always try to make people aware of the environment and how important it is for us to care for our world and all living things.

5. In many ways, Francis was ahead of his time. He should have been the first saint to earn his own Green Flag!

Time for reflection

We all think about recycling and saving energy, but what can we do to help animals and small creatures? Francis had no interest in money or possessions. What things do we enjoy that cannot be bought?

Prayer
We thank you for our world. Help us to care for it and make sure that it can be enjoyed by those who come after us.
Amen

Song

'Make me a channel of your peace' – based on a prayer attributed to Francis (*Come and Praise*, 147)

EPIPHANY
The coming of the wise men
(6 January)

By Rebecca Parkinson

Suitable for whole school

Aim

To learn about the festival of Epiphany and what it means to Christians.

Preparation and materials

- **Background** The traditional date for Epiphany is 6 January – the twelfth day after Christmas – but, in many countries, it is now observed on the first Sunday that falls between 2 and 8 January.
- **Props** Collect together a range of objects that could be given as presents to different people. For example, a baby's toy for a baby, a doll for a young child, a mobile phone for a variety of people, men's and ladies' clothes and so on. In the assembly the children will be asked to guess who might receive each gift. Also, think of and/or bring in a present you have received at some time that was a complete surprise to you. Alternatively, ask another member of staff if they have ever received a surprise present and ask them to share the story of this with the children. You will also need a dictionary, to look up the word 'Epiphany'. Write the definitions on pieces of paper: 1) 'the manifestation of Christ to the Gentiles as represented by the Magi (Matthew 2.1–12)'; 2) 'a moment of sudden and great revelation' (*Concise Oxford English Dictionary*).

Assembly

1. Explain to the children that, as it has recently been Christmas, you are going to show them a few different presents and ask them to guess who might like to receive them – a man, woman, child, grown-up, an old person. Show the presents one at a time and ask the children who it would be suitable

for and why. Ask them why you wouldn't give certain presents to certain people – why you wouldn't give an old man a baby toy, for instance.

2. Ask the children if any of them would like to share their stories about a special present they received at Christmas. Remind them that a special present doesn't have to be big or expensive – it may just be something you really wanted, or from a special person.

3. Share – or ask other members of staff to share – a story about receiving a present that was a complete surprise. This may have been when you or they were a child or an adult; it may have been for Christmas or birthday or even when you got engaged or some other special time.

4. Explain that on 6 January each year Christians celebrate a special festival called Epiphany. Epiphany celebrates the wise men visiting baby Jesus. Ask the children if they can remember anyone else who visited baby Jesus – hopefully someone will say the shepherds! Explain that there were lots of differences between the shepherds and the wise men – see if the children can think of any. Examples would be that the shepherds were poor, but the wise men were rich and the shepherds came from the same country as Jesus and were Jews, but the wise men came from a different country and were Gentiles. 'Gentile' means a non-Jewish person. In Jesus' day, Jews and Gentiles didn't ever mix with each other. Also, the shepherds were in the fields close by, but the wise men travelled a long way. Another difference is that the angels appeared to the shepherds, but the wise men followed a star.

5. Explain that all these differences show us that God wanted everyone to see baby Jesus. In God's eyes, it doesn't matter if we are rich or poor or what country we come from.

6. Explain to the children that, just as the gifts you showed them at the start of the assembly were special for somebody, the wise men brought three special gifts as presents for Jesus. These gifts were gold, frankincense and myrrh. Christians believe that the three gifts each had a meaning. You may like to ask the children if they can guess what each gift could mean. Gold recognized that Jesus was a king. Frankincense is a special kind of fragrance that was used by priests, often to represent prayer. Myrrh indicated that Jesus was to die –

people at that time used it to anoint the dead, ready for burial.

7. Ask someone to look up the first definition of Epiphany in the dictionary and someone else to hold up that definition you wrote on the first piece of paper: 'the manifestation of Christ to the Gentiles as represented by the Magi (Matthew 2.1–12)'. Explain that the feast of Epiphany recalls the visit of the wise men and their gifts.

8. Ask someone to look up the second definition of Epiphany in the dictionary and someone else to hold up the definition you wrote on the other piece of paper: 'a moment of sudden and great revelation'. Explain that, at the time Jesus was born, Jews and Gentiles (non-Jews) never mixed. It would have been a hugely surprising revelation that God wanted Gentiles (wise men) to see a Jewish baby (Jesus). The feast of Epiphany reminds us that God doesn't have favourites but welcomes people from any background and any nationality.

Time for reflection

The wise men must have been quite rich to bring such special gifts to Jesus. Even though it isn't recorded in the Bible, it is possible that the shepherds also brought gifts. A famous Christmas carol – 'In the bleak midwinter' – has this verse about bringing gifts to Jesus:

> What can I give him, poor as I am?
> If I were a shepherd, I would bring a lamb.
> If I were a wise man, I would do my part.
> Yet what I can I give him: give my heart.

Think about those words. What do they mean to you?

Prayer
Thank you that you wanted both rich and poor to see you.
Thank you that, as we think about Epiphany, we are reminded that every person is important to you. Please help us to use all the gifts that you have given to us.
Thank you for all these good things.
Amen

Song

'The wise may bring their learning' (*Come and Praise*, 64)

CANDLEMAS
Jesus' presentation at the temple ceremony remembered
(2 February or nearest Sunday)

By John Challis

Suitable for whole school

Aim

To learn to look past the visible and see the hidden parts of Jesus.

Preparation and materials

- **Background** At Candlemas, Christians remember Mary taking baby Jesus to the temple to be presented to God. Two elderly people, Simeon and Anna, are presented with a baby, but they recognize the Messiah. This will be both good news and sad news because Jesus will die for all. Candlemas often has the theme of being sweet and sour.
- **Props** Buy around five pieces of fruit – a banana, an apple, a pear, a satsuma and a lemon. Carefully prise off the tip or tiny part of the lemon's stalk that is left at one end of the lemon, and then take a crisp £5 note, roll it very tightly and slide it into the lemon. It should easily fill the length of the lemon. Replace the tip, if you can, with glue. This is an old magician's trick. You will also need a small chopping board, a knife to cut the lemon and a biscuit.

Assembly

1. Explain to the children that Candlemas is when Christians remember Mary taking baby Jesus to the temple to be presented to God. Baby Jesus was presented to two elderly people, Simeon and Anna. This is both a great moment to celebrate, and sad. Simeon and Anna are prophets who had been waiting for God to send his Messiah, his special messenger. They see baby Jesus but they also see so much more in him.

2. Ask the children, 'Who likes fruit?' Then, show the fruit that you have brought and ask the children, 'Who would like to eat some here and now?' With your volunteers at the front, let them choose their fruit. Each in turn will take a bite, but the child with the lemon will wait. Build the tension, saying how awful it is to eat a lemon; compare the tastes and so on. The other children will describe, perhaps with your help, the sweet tastes of the other fruits.

3. Say to the child with the lemon, 'Would you prefer to have a biscuit or a piece of one of the other fruits?' Play on this and enjoy trying to convince him or her to have the biscuit or another fruit or the lemon.

4. Ask the other children to return to their places with their fruit, thanking them.

   Bring out the chopping board and build up to cutting the lemon so that the child can eat it. Alternatively, if they decided to take the other fruit or the biscuit, say that you still want to cut up the lemon.

5. Cut the lemon around the widest part, being careful not to go in too deep, and the lemon should divide into two halves easily (twist it if it doesn't), leaving the rolled-up £5 note in the middle. Ask the child to take the note out if he or she had agreed to eat the lemon or, if the child had left it for you to eat, then show the children, with a look of shock and amazement, and say, 'Even in the sourest of things, like a lemon, there can be the sweetest of surprises – a £5 note!' The children will be surprised and wonder how it came to be there. You can then either give the lemon and the £5 note to the student or keep it and say that Candlemas is also seen as being sweet and sour – sweet and good that Jesus was born to show us what God is like, but sour and bad as he died on the cross, but sweet and so good again because he rose to new life with God.

Time for reflection

Sometimes it is too easy to look past the visible and miss the invisible treasures within. We judge from the outside, but even when things don't look good, there can be a great reward inside.

Prayer
Give us the eyes of faith, to see you in the world.
Where fear closes our eyes, help us.
Where tears blind us, heal us.
Set us free to see your love at work in the world.
Amen

🎵 Song

'Light up the fire' (*Come and Praise*, 55)

CORPUS CHRISTI
The body of Christ (Thursday after Trinity Sunday – movable festival)

By Laurence Chilcott

Suitable for Key Stage 2

Aims

To relate our experience of special meals to the last meal that Jesus shared with his disciples and to understand the special significance it has for Christians.

Preparation and materials

- **Background** The feast of Corpus Christi is a Christian festival marking the 'real presence of Christ' in the Eucharist – also known as Holy Communion, the Lord's Supper, Mass – held on the Thursday after Trinity Sunday. The Catholic Church of England and Wales celebrates this feast on the following Sunday. The Church of England also marks it as a way of thanking God for Holy Communion.
- **Props** Display pictures of people sharing meals in various situations – at a restaurant, a birthday party, wedding and so on – and a picture of *The Last Supper* by Leonardo da Vinci.

Assembly

1. I wonder how many of you today will have at least one of your meals on your lap in front of the television. Perhaps breakfast was like that. Some of you will have come to school early and had something at the breakfast club. Everybody seems to be so busy these days that families do not always get the chance to sit down together at mealtimes.

   There will be some special times, though, when every family, no matter how busy, will find time to sit around a table together to share a special meal. It may be for a birthday, Christmas or Eid *(if you have children from other faiths, insert their key festivals here)*, it may be for a special occasion or anniversary. On such occasions we get the opportunity to talk together, share the best food we can afford and enjoy one another's company. Sometimes these mealtimes will be remembered for years to come – it may be because of the people who were there with you or, perhaps, because of something that happened at the time.

2. The last meal that Jesus shared with his special friends, the disciples, was one such occasion. The meal was held in an upstairs room in a house in Jerusalem where they met to celebrate the Passover. It also gave them a chance to get away from the crowds who followed Jesus wherever he went. They were all there – even Judas, who was later to betray Jesus to the authorities.

   It began in a rather strange way when Jesus, their leader, washed the feet of each one of the disciples in turn. Now this was not unusual as they lived in a hot country where people generally wore sandals and the roads were dusty – but it was a servant's job, certainly not something a leader would do. Jesus explained that his followers should think of others more than themselves, they should not behave as if they were better than others, but be prepared to act like servants and help anyone in need.

   It was in this room that Jesus talked about how he would soon be captured and put to death. He even told them that one of the friends in that room had already planned to turn him over to the authorities, who wanted to arrest him. Even so, he still wanted to spend this special time with them all, so sat at the table that had been prepared for them.

   It was a simple meal. It started with bread, which Jesus broke and shared out with his friends. As he gave it to them, he said, 'This is my body that is given for you.' Then he poured out the wine and said, 'This is my blood that is poured out for the forgiveness of sins.' *(You might want to explain these expressions.)*

   Although they did not realize it at the time, this was the last meal that Jesus would have with all his disciples. Soon he would be arrested, beaten and mocked by his captors and put to death on a cross like a common criminal. Only afterwards, when Jesus rose from the dead, did they understand just how important that last evening meal, or supper, was.

3. All over the world, Christian churches remember that last meal in a service sometimes called 'The Lord's Supper', 'Holy Communion', 'Mass', the 'Eucharist'. Those who take part share bread and wine just as Jesus did that evening and remember what he said to his friends. Not all churches celebrate it in quite the same way, but for all Christians it is a very special and solemn part of the service.

4. Corpus Christi means 'the body of Christ', and this festival remembers especially how it is represented in the Eucharist. For the Catholic Church it is often marked by a short or longer procession of church members through the streets of a town or city. A priest leads the procession, carrying the bread used for the Eucharist in a special, decorated container to display it, called a monstrance. After processing through the streets they may return to the church they started out from or go to another church for the rest of the service.

5. Corpus Christi gives Christians the opportunity to focus their thoughts on the body of Jesus Christ and how he gave it for us.

Time for reflection

Look at the picture of *The Last Supper*. Which one do you think is Jesus? How many disciples are there? Which one do you think is Judas? What do you think Jesus has just said to them?

Think of a meal that you remember as being very special. Who was with you?

What was the occasion? What made it especially memorable?

Prayer
We thank you for the special times we share with our families and friends. Thank you for the food we enjoy and the fun we have.
Amen

Song

'The Lord's Prayer' (*Come and Praise*, 51)

LENT
Jesus fasting in the desert
(spring – movable festival)

By Rebecca Parkinson

Suitable for whole school

Aim

To consider the meaning of the Christian season of Lent.

Preparation and materials

- **Props** Large card with 'Be prepared' written on it. A number of cards on which are written situations that we need to prepare for, such as, 'Going on holiday', 'A friend staying for a sleepover', 'Taking a ballet or music exam', 'Playing a football match', 'Being in the Olympics', 'A school play'.

Assembly

1. Ask the children what they did before they came to school this morning. As they each say what they did, ask them if they could come to the front and mime that action – for example, waking up, getting out of bed, getting dressed, having a wash, eating breakfast, packing their bag, brushing their teeth, putting on their coat, walking to school. Eventually, ask all the children at the front to carry out their actions at the same time. Pretend to be surprised at what a lot of 'preparation' has gone into their simply arriving at school!

2. Ask if any of the children are in the Beavers, Scouts or Rainbows, Brownies or Guides. Ask them what their promise or motto is. The Beavers' and Rainbows' promise is 'To do my best'. The Brownies' motto is 'Lend a hand' and the Scouts' is 'Be prepared'. Ask a child to hold up the card with 'Be prepared' written on it.

3. Ask for a volunteer to hold up the first of your situation cards. Ask the children what preparations they would need to make

for that event. For example, for 'Going on holiday', they would need to book somewhere to stay, maybe book a flight, pack and so on. Discuss each card, then ask what would happen if they made no preparations.

4. Tell the children that the festival we are thinking about today is called Lent. It is a time when Christians remember the preparations that Jesus went through.

5. For 30 years of his life, Jesus lived at home in Nazareth. At the age of 30, Jesus knew that he was about to start his public work. He was about to start teaching people about God and perform many amazing miracles. He knew that it would not be easy and, eventually, would lead to his death. In preparation for this time, Jesus went to be baptized by John the Baptist and then off on his own into the desert for 40 days. For 40 days and nights he fasted, which means that he didn't eat or drink anything. During this time he was tempted to do a number of things that he knew it was wrong to do. Jesus didn't give in to temptation and didn't do anything wrong. At the end of the 40 days, Jesus left the desert and began the work he had come to Earth to do. His time in the desert prepared him for this.

6. Lent is the period of time that leads up to Easter. It begins on Ash Wednesday (the day after Shrove Tuesday when, traditionally, pancakes are cooked). For Christians, Easter is the most important time of the year – it is then that they remember the death and resurrection of Jesus. Because Christians want to 'Be prepared' for the celebration of Easter, they use Lent as a time to think more about God, go to special church services and pray.

7. Lent lasts for 40 days and nights (not including Sundays) – the same length of time that Jesus spent in the desert preparing for his work. The idea is that Lent focuses Christians' minds on God, but also helps them to think of others who are not as fortunate as they are.

8. As part of Lent, Christians often give up something for 40 days, just as Jesus fasted, going without food, in the desert. Commonly people give up chocolate, smoking, watching TV. In recent years there has been a move towards doing something positive during Lent instead of giving something up, such as collecting for a charity, tidying your room, saying

something encouraging to someone every day, making your bed, doing homework without complaining!
9. Ask the children if they can think of any other ideas that would be positive things they could do during Lent.
10. For Christians, Lent leads them into Easter – the highlight of the Christian calendar.

Time for reflection

Traditionally, people have given things up for Lent, but more recently many choose to do something positive. Ask the children, 'Can you think of something special that you could do during Lent that would help someone else?

Suggest that they could use the time to help raise money for a school charity to help people in another country who are not as well off as we are. Maybe they could decide to give someone a compliment each day!

Experts tell us that if you do something for 40 days, it will become a habit that you do automatically without thinking about it. Wouldn't it be good if Lent helped the children to carry on doing something positive for the rest of the year?

> *Prayer*
> Thank you that, in the busyness of life, there are times to stop and think.
> Help us never to be so busy that we don't have time to be peaceful and silent.
> Thank you for times such as Lent that remind us to think about you and to consider what we can do to help those less fortunate than we are.
> Please help us always to 'Be prepared' to help other people.
> **Amen**

Song

'One more step' (*Come and Praise*, 47)

ASCENSION
Jesus says goodbye to his friends and ascends into heaven (Thursday, 40 days after Easter – movable festival)

By Laurence Chilcott

Suitable for whole school

Aim

To consider how we feel when we lose a very good friend, and relate that to the time when Jesus left his disciples and returned to heaven.

Preparation and materials

- **Background** Christians celebrate the time when Jesus went back up into heaven, called Ascension because he 'ascended'. Ascension occurs 40 days after Easter, on a Thursday, and many churches hold special services to celebrate this event in the life of Jesus. The Catholic Church in England and Wales usually celebrates it on the Sunday following. In Scandinavian countries, the Netherlands and Germany, schoolchildren have a holiday on this day.
- **Props** Display pictures of people saying goodbye – waving from a train, hugging each other, wiping away a tear, evacuees leaving home and so on.

Assembly

1. Friends are very important to us. Sometimes, especially at school, we will have a special friend whom we call our 'best friend'. Best friends spend as much time as possible together and, at special times like birthday parties, sleepovers or trips to the cinema, they will be first on the invitation list. Best friends help one another and give support in difficult times; they are loyal and can be trusted.

2. Imagine how you would feel if your best friend had to move away and would no longer be going to the same school as you. Who would you sit next to on the school trip? Who would be your partner in PE? Who would you play with at breaktime? No doubt you would feel it was just not fair, but you would also understand that you couldn't do anything about it.

    Eventually, the time would come for you to say goodbye. You'd promise to keep in touch, perhaps arrange to visit one another in the school holidays, but you would feel a real sense of loss. You would be left wondering if your friendship can stay strong when you won't see each other almost every day.

3. The Bible says that Jesus had a group of special friends – the disciples – and they thought of him as their best friend. For two to three years they had travelled around the country together, sharing meals and talking long into the night. He had amazed them with miracles of healing, he had taught them many things and explained how God loved them, but one day he told them that he would soon have to leave them. They couldn't believe it – they just didn't want to lose their best friend.

    Not long after Jesus had spoken about leaving them, it happened – and it was a nightmare! Judas, who had been one of the group, betrayed Jesus and led the authorities to him. The friends were with Jesus when they arrested him, but they weren't very good friends – they ran away. One of them, Peter, followed the guards who arrested Jesus at a distance, but he pretended he didn't even know Jesus when a servant girl asked if he was his friend. Jesus was left to face his captors alone, deserted by his friends. He was cruelly treated, subjected to a mocking trial and eventually crucified, which means that he was put to death on a cross.

    When Jesus was crucified, the friends were devastated – they realized that they had let him down and regretted how they had not tried to do something to help him. They were afraid that they, too, might be arrested and were confused about what to do, now Jesus was dead.

    On Easter Sunday, however, Jesus rose from the dead and was seen by some of his friends. They could hardly believe it, but it was indeed their friend Jesus, they had no doubt about that. He was different in some ways, but that didn't matter, for their friend had returned to them.

Although they didn't realize it, Jesus wasn't back for good. For 40 days, Jesus appeared to many people in many different places, but one day he took them up to a mountain and talked to them for the last time. Jesus told them that they were to tell people about God's love for the world and how he had been raised from the dead according to God's plan. He knew it wasn't going to be easy, but he promised that he would send the Holy Spirit to help them. Then, suddenly, he was taken from their sight – ascending, being lifted up to heaven to return to his Father.

So when it seemed as if they had just got their friend back, he left them again. They didn't know what the future held and wondered how they could face life without their leader. All they could do was go to Jerusalem as Jesus had instructed and wait for the Holy Spirit to come. That Spirit did come . . . it's a story for another day. *(See Pentecost, overleaf.)*

Time for reflection

Do you have something that reminds you of a special friend? It may be a gift that he or she gave you for your birthday or perhaps a photograph of you together. Although, as you grow up, your friends may change and keepsakes are lost or mislaid, you will always have the memories of your friends at school. Think about one of your best friends and what makes him or her special to you.

Jesus' friends, his disciples, had only memories about their time with him. It is from what they remembered and told others or what they wrote themselves that we have the accounts of Jesus' life today in the New Testament.

Prayer
We thank you for friends whom we will always remember, even if they are no longer with us. We are thankful that you have promised to be a friend to us and ask that you will show us how to be loyal and true friends at all times.
Amen

Song

'The best gift' (*Come and Praise*, 59)

PENTECOST
Beginning of the Christian Church (Sunday, 50 days after Easter – movable festival)

By Laurence Chilcott

Suitable for whole school

Aims

To consider the coming of the Holy Spirit from Peter's point of view and relate this to the beginning of the Christian Church.

Preparation and materials

- **Background** The Christian Church celebrates Pentecost on the Sunday 50 days after Easter Sunday. It denotes the time when the Holy Spirit, promised by Jesus, came to the apostles who were waiting in Jerusalem. It marks the beginning of the Christian Church, for it was after this time that Jesus' followers began to preach the gospel, or good news of Jesus' resurrection and promise of forgiveness and eternal life for his followers.
- **Props** Display some of the symbols associated with the Holy Spirit – fire, wind, water, a dove, light. You can then explain or have a sheet with the explanation written down, saying we sometimes find it hard to put into ordinary words an experience that is extraordinary, and these symbols have been used to represent just that sort of experience, to get the message across.
- You might prepare a class to mime the story, with Peter narrating, or a display of pictures or a tableau to illustrate Peter's thoughts.

Assembly

Tell the children the following story.

Peter's story

Peter stood in the middle of the room and wept. Everything came flooding back to him. This was the room where he had shared the last meal with Jesus and his friends. He had sat on that very chair and Jesus had washed his feet. How could their leader act like a servant and wash their hot, dusty feet? Peter thought about what Jesus had said and done on that night and realized that only now was he beginning to understand.

He recalled how he had told Jesus that he was prepared to die protecting him – then had let him down when Jesus was arrested. He had been so scared that he, too, might be arrested, he followed Jesus and his captors, but kept well out of sight. He remembered how he had denied that he was one of Jesus' friends – not once, but three times. Peter blushed with shame just thinking about it. How could he have talked so bravely yet acted like a coward?

Things had changed since and now he knew he had a fresh start. Jesus had risen from the dead and made it clear that he had forgiven Peter for letting him down. He had even told Peter that there was important work for him to do. Jesus had gone back to his father in heaven, but before he went, told his disciples to go to Jerusalem and wait for the Holy Spirit to come.

Hearing the footsteps of the other disciples on the stairs, Peter drew his sleeve across his face, hoping no one would notice that he had been crying. They joined Peter, who was thankful no one did notice, and soon the conversation turned to what they should do now that they were together again.

Although Peter could be a bit headstrong, saying or doing things without thinking first, the disciples looked up to him and soon they were following his lead. Peter was impatient to begin the work that Jesus had set him to do, but the problem was that he knew he had to wait until the Holy Spirit came – and he wasn't going to let Jesus down again by not doing as he had asked. Peter wondered how the Holy Spirit would come, but he didn't have to wait long before he found out . . .

It started with a sound like the wind. It grew louder and louder until he could hardly bear it. The other disciples could hear it too – you could see that from the looks on their faces! The whole house seemed to be filled with the sound. Then – and he could hardly believe what he was seeing – flames of fire appeared in the room, separating out and touching, but not burning, the heads of each one of them.

That's what he saw – or at least that's the only way he could describe what he saw – but how he felt was even more amazing. It was as if Jesus had come to him again, but not just into the room – it was as if he was right inside him.

So this was the Holy Spirit! Jesus in another form and he would never leave him now. Peter realized that, while Jesus could only be in one place at one time, his Holy Spirit could be with him wherever he went.

Everyone in the room with Peter had exactly the same experience and they just had to go outside to tell someone – and there were plenty of people to tell. As it was Pentecost, a harvest celebration, Jerusalem was full of visitors from all around the world. It wasn't only Peter who wanted to talk – all the disciples wanted to join in and the people in the street couldn't help but listen, so a crowd quickly gathered. The disciples were so excited and filled with the Holy Spirit that they all started speaking at once – to some people they just seemed to be gabbling and talking nonsense, but it soon became clear that they were speaking in different languages so that even the foreign visitors to Jerusalem could understand them. With the disciples all talking at the same time – some getting excited, raising their voices and waving their arms about – it was hardly surprising that someone in the crowd said, 'They must be drunk!'

It was then that Peter took control and quietened the disciples so that he could speak to the crowds himself. First of all, he told them how it was too early in the day for them to be drunk, then he told them about the good news: that Jesus had risen from the dead to demonstrate God's love and power. Peter explained how they could join with them and experience God's Holy Spirit for themselves and, by the end of that day, around 3,000 people had become followers of Jesus. This was the start of the Christian Church, which grew and spread throughout the whole world.

Time for reflection

Although Peter had let Jesus down, Jesus forgave him and gave him a second chance. Are we prepared to give people a second chance if they have said they are sorry for hurting or upsetting us?

Think of the best or most exciting experience you have had. What would you draw to show how you felt right inside you at the time?

Prayer
Help us to remember that you have promised to be with us, wherever we are. Give us the strength to stand up for what is right, help those who are in need and, by our actions, follow the example of Jesus.
Amen

Song

'Spirit of God' (*Come and Praise*, 63)

IGNATIUS OF LOYOLA (31 July)

By Rebecca Parkinson

Suitable for whole school

Aim

To learn about Ignatius of Loyola, the founder of the Jesuit movement.

Preparation and materials

- **Props** Whiteboard or flipchart to write on.

Assembly

1. Ask one of the younger children for the name of your school and write it on the whiteboard or flipchart. Now ask the children if they know the names of any other local schools – primary or secondary. Record, or ask the children to record, these on the board or chart.

2. Explain to them that you are going to tell them about a boy who grew up to be responsible for the formation of many schools all over the world.

   The story of Ignatius of Loyola
   Ignatius was born in Spain in 1491. He was the youngest of 13 children and, when he was only 7 years old, his mother died. A short while later, Ignatius became a pageboy (a type of servant) and, following that, at the age of 18, he became a soldier.

   Ignatius was a good soldier and considered very brave by the men he fought alongside. Some 12 years after joining the army, however, he was seriously injured when a cannonball broke one of his legs and seriously injured the other. Ignatius was recovering in hospital for a long time, during which he asked if he could be brought something to read. He was given a book about the life of Jesus and some stories about the lives of different saints.

These stories had a huge impact on Ignatius and he decided that he would dedicate the rest of his life to God – but there was a problem. In those days, priests were expected to speak to people in Latin, the Bible could only be read in Latin and church services could only be conducted in Latin. Ignatius could not speak a word of Latin!

So he decided to go back to school. He was 33 years old when he joined a class that was made up of 10-year-old boys. He was laughed at and found it difficult, but he was determined to succeed – and, eventually, he did. It took him ten years to become a priest.

After this, Ignatius gathered a group of nine friends and, together, they set off to travel the world, telling people about God wherever they went. Ignatius had an exciting life. Many people began to follow God because of him and sometimes countries welcomed him, sometimes they didn't. He wrote a number of books and spent some time in prison because of what he believed.

Over time, many people began to follow Ignatius' teaching. They became known as Jesuits. When Ignatius got older and couldn't travel so easily, he spent his time sending other Jesuits to different parts of the world – to tell people about God, but also set up schools and colleges. Ignatius thought that teaching children about God was a vital part of their education.

3. Today, Jesuits form the largest single order of priests and brothers in the Roman Catholic Church. There are 240 Jesuit universities and colleges and 700 secondary schools throughout the world, not to mention primary schools and other services they offer to the poor and others in need.

Jesuits, therefore, are still involved in education all over the world, so many people have been influenced by the life of Ignatius of Loyola. He died on 31 July 1556 and Jesuits remember him on this, his feast day.

4. So we can see that Ignatius thought he had his life mapped out in front him – but things went wrong! When he was badly injured, he could have been miserable, blamed God and given up. Instead, he began to follow God's plan for his life and was brave enough to take the action needed to change how he lived. It must have been very hard for him to go back to school

with ten-year-olds, but he was determined to do this and succeeded.

5. What do we do when things go wrong in our lives? Do we grumble and complain and feel sorry for ourselves? Ignatius shows us that we should never give up hope because positive things can still come out of bad situations. We need to have a positive attitude and grasp every opportunity we get in life!

Time for reflection

Ignatius wrote these words to God:

> Give me only your love and your grace. With this I am rich enough and I have no more to ask.

Stop for a moment and think about your day so far. Can you think of a time when you have already complained because things haven't quite gone as you wanted? Maybe you didn't want to get up! Maybe what you would have liked for breakfast wasn't available. Maybe something went wrong in the playground. Let's ask God to help our attitudes to be like Ignatius of Loyola's – always looking for the best in every situation and always being satisfied with what we have.

Prayer
When things go wrong, help us to realize that you are always there. Even when we don't understand why things happen, help us to know that you have a plan for our lives.
Thank you for the work of Ignatius of Loyola.
Thank you that, because of the things he did during his life, so many people still benefit today.
Please help us to live our lives in a way that benefits other people.
Amen

Song

'Go, tell it on the mountain' (*Come and Praise*, 24)

4
HINDUISM

DIWALI
Festival of lights (October/ November – movable festival)

By Alan M. Barker

Suitable for whole school

Aims

To mark the festival of Diwali and reflect on its significance.

Preparation and materials

- **Background** Diwali (also spelt Divali) means 'row of lights'. Diwali is a festival lasting from one to five days. It is celebrated by Hindus and Sikhs at a time of the darkest night of the lunar month. For many Hindus, Diwali is a New Year festival and originates in celebrations of the end of the monsoon season in India. It is also the beginning of a new business year and prayers are said for a prosperous new year. Rituals and celebrations vary from region to region, but the lighting of diva lamps (traditionally, earthenware bowls filled with oil or butter, called ghee, with cotton wicks) is universal. The lamps symbolize the triumph of good over bad, light over darkness. Two stories are often told: the return of Rama, Sita, Lakshmana and Hanuman to Ayodhya after the defeat of the demon Ravana, and the story of Lakshmi (goddess of wealth and prosperity), who traditionally blesses homes in which lamps have been lit to greet her. This assembly tells the story of Rama, Sita, Lakshmana and Hanuman.
- **Props** A small torch or key fob light, eight tealights in suitable and safe holders, and means to light them, images of Diwali celebrations (these can be found on the internet, but check regarding copyright). Note that the story of Rama, Sita, Lakshmana and Hanuman might be enacted by a group of children, told using PowerPoint slides or, for a fuller version, Anita Ganeri's *The Diwali Story* (Evans, 2003) could be read out.
- To ascertain the date of Diwali, visit <www.bbc.co.uk/religion/tools/calendar>.

Pronunciation notes (local pronunciations may vary):

Diwali	di-vaa-lee or di-waa-lee
Rama	raa-ma
Sita	see-ta
Lakshmana	lack-shmana

Assembly

1. Introduce the theme of light by commenting that evenings are growing darker and, in unlit areas, a small torch or key light is helpful to find your way home.

2. Reflect that light is the theme of a religious festival called Diwali (also spelt Divali). It's celebrated by Hindus on the darkest night around the end of October, which originates in celebrations of the end of the monsoon season in India, and is often known as the 'festival of lights'.

3. Explain that Diwali is a joyful occasion. Invite any children who are Hindus to describe the celebrations that take place. Families clean and decorate their homes in preparation. Streets and buildings are decorated with lights. Cards are sent and gifts exchanged. Special food and sweets are enjoyed and fireworks are often set off as part of the celebrations. Everyone prays for prosperity and good fortune in the days that lie ahead. Most especially, small lamps, called divas, are lit.

4. This tradition arises from the story of Rama, Sita, Lakshmana and Hanuman, which is retold each year during Diwali.

   The story of Rama, Sita, Lakshmana and Hanuman
   Rama was a prince who married a beautiful princess, Sita. His father wanted Rama to become king, but his mother didn't agree. She wanted Rama's brother, Bharat, to have that honour.

   Rama and Sita were told that they must leave the kingdom for 14 years. Another brother, Lakshmana, went with them.

   Eventually, the old king died. Knowing and honouring his father's wishes, Bharat went to the far-off forest, where he found the other members of his family and invited them to return, but they had promised to stay away for 14 years and Rama insisted that they must be true to their word. So they stayed in the forest where, one day, an evil demon named

Ravana captured Sita and carried her off to an island. She was imprisoned in his palace.

Rama and Lakshmana searched for her and a bird told them where she was being held. With the help of Hanuman, the monkey general, Rama went to the castle, where there was a huge battle. Eventually, Rama killed the demon king with a golden arrow and Sita was rescued.

As the 14 years had passed, it was time for Rama to return home. As their journey neared its end, the night was very dark, with no moon to light the path ahead. So to help the new King Rama and Queen Sita find their way, all their people placed small lamps outside their houses. Explain that this is one of the reasons lamps are lit every year at the time of Diwali.

5. Reflect that the story of Rama, Sita, Lakshmana and Hanuman tells how good can triumph over evil. It shows how friendship can provide help and support during dark and difficult times. (You could ask, 'Who proved to be good friends in the story? Who may prove to be a good friend in school today?') Faith and friendship can help us to find our true destiny.

Time for reflection

Conclude by dimming the lights and slowly light the tealights, one by one. Then invite everyone to reflect on the story of Rama, Sita, Lakshmana and Hanuman.

It speaks of the importance of friendship and loyalty, giving and sharing, goodness and happiness, hope and new beginnings.

Wish everyone a happy Diwali.

Song

'Flickering candles in the night' (*Come and Praise 2*, 114)

GANESH CHATURTHI
Birthday of the elephant-headed god (August/September – movable festival)

By Alan M. Barker

Suitable for Key Stage 2

Aim

To consider how to overcome obstacles with reference to the Hindu god, Ganesha.

Preparation and materials

- **Background** Be aware that children will vary in how well they know this story and what version they know – the celebration of this festival and accounts of the story of Ganesha vary in different parts of India and among Hindu communities around the world. The festival lasts for about seven to ten days and is held between mid-August and mid-September, with the exact date fixed by the lunar calendar. It therefore either slightly precedes or follows the start of the autumn term in the UK.
- **Props** An image or statue of the elephant-headed god, Ganesha, images of elephants at work (optional), PowerPoint slides to display key phrases – 'Stop and think', 'Don't rush', 'Take one step at a time', 'Don't panic', 'Keep trying', 'Ask for help', for example – around an appropriate image (optional).
- To ascertain the date of Ganesh Chaturthi, visit <www.bbc.co.uk/religion/tools/calendar>.

Pronunciation notes (local pronunciations may vary):

| Ganesh Chaturthi | ga-nesh cha-ter-thee |
| Parvati | par-va-tee |

Assembly

1. Introduce the image of the god Ganesha. He will be recognized by those of Hindu faith who celebrate his birthday during the festival of Ganesh Chaturthi.

2. Say that the appearance of Ganesha is explained by a sacred story, of which there are many different versions.

    One of the commonest stories is that, in a fit of temper, the god Shiva cut off the child Ganesha's head. Little did he know that Ganesha was a child created by his lovely wife, Parvati. Shiva went into the forest searching for a new head for his son. An elephant was the first creature he saw. He used the head to restore Ganesha to life. Parvati was pleased. 'Now Ganesha will be strong and wise', she said.

3. Refer to how the strength of elephants is used in some parts of Asia to complete difficult tasks, such as removing logs from dense plantations. The age to which elephants live is thought to make them wise. They are creatures that move slowly and thoughtfully. It's said that 'elephants never forget'.

4. Continue by saying that Hindus believe Ganesha is a very special god. He is the god of beginnings and is thought to be able to remove obstacles. (The word 'obstacle' can be explained by reference to an obstacle race – an obstacle is a challenge or difficulty that gets in the way and stops progress.) Prayers are offered to Ganesha when people start a journey or make other new beginnings.

5. Focus on the obstacles that your school community might encounter at the beginning of the new term or during their daily learning. Reflect that we all get stuck sometimes and that new beginnings aren't always easy. Invite the school community to consider ways in which obstacles can be removed and overcome.

6. If using PowerPoint slides, display the key words, phrases and images you have put together.

7. Affirm the effectiveness of such an approach. Acknowledge that, while obstacles can't always be removed, often they are not quite as big or impossible to deal with as we imagine.

8. Alternatively, conclude with the following story, told as a warning, should anyone ever be tempted to laugh at another person's difficulty. Ganesha was well known for his enormous appetite. Once he ate so much at a feast that he couldn't stand up! As he struggled to his feet, the moon began to laugh. Ganesha was so angry that he cursed the moon and everyone looking at it. As a result, in some places, people

believe that it's unlucky to look at the moon on Ganesha Chaturthi, the birthday of the elephant-headed god.

Time for reflection

Reflect that it's certainly unkind and unwise to laugh at anyone who is struggling with difficulty. Like Ganesha, we should help one another to overcome obstacles. Invite the children to think or pray quietly. Introduce this thought:

> A long journey is made up of many small steps – and the first step towards overcoming an obstacle is to believe that we can!

Songs

'When I needed a neighbour' (*Come and Praise*, 65)

'Give it all you've got!' (*Songs for Every Assembly*, Out of the Ark Music)

HOLI
Festival of colour (February/March – movable festival)

By Alan M. Barker

Suitable for Key Stage 2

Aim

To explore the significance of the Hindu festival of Holi.

Preparation and materials

- **Background** Holi is a springtime festival celebrated on full moon day in the month of Phalunga in the Indian national calendar. This usually coincides with the month of March. It is celebrated in different ways, but some of the common features are the harvesting of winter crops and building a bonfire on which coconut and grains are roasted and shared as prasada (holy food). Often, young children and babies are carried around the bonfire as it is thought that it will offer them protection from harm. The image of fire is linked to the story of Prahlada and Holika (see below). The celebrations are deliberately riotous, for example throwing coloured water and powders. This is linked with the themes of spring and fertility and can also be traced back to the god Krishna, who liked to play practical jokes and had coloured water thrown over him by a milkmaid. Very often at Holi, people will play practical jokes on one another. It's a festival of great variety and great fun.
- **Props** Obtain some suitable, copyright-free images of Holi celebrations from the internet and encourage the children, ahead of the assembly, to create splatter paintings or prepare one large canvas to create a colourful display.

    The school might be invited to mark Holi by wearing brightly coloured T-shirts.
- To ascertain the date of Holi, visit <www.bbc.co.uk/religion/tools/calendar>.

Pronunciation notes (local pronunciations may vary):

Holi	holy
Gopis	go-pees
Prahlada	praa-lada
Holika	ho-lee-ka

Assembly

1. Display the splatter painting or paintings. You can say that, although they don't look like anything, they express mood and energy. In conversation, invite the children who produced the paintings to reflect their feelings about their work. Observe that splatter painting is energetic and fun!

2. Explain that, especially in Northern India, Hindu communities mark springtime with the happy and colourful festival of Holi. The exact celebrations vary from place to place, but everywhere they are filled with colour and fun. Display the images of Holi to demonstrate how friends and families cover themselves and others (even strangers!) with brightly coloured water and powders. No one is upset because everyone understands that it is Holi, a time of happiness and celebration.

3. During Holi, some recall the playfulness of the god Krishna, who was very mischievous when he was young. It's said that, when tending his cows, he played practical jokes on the gopis, or milkmaids, and they threw coloured water over him. Observe that, as we grow older, it's important that we learn to act responsibly. It's also important, though, that we keep our sense of humour and continue to enjoy play.

4. Younger children might be reminded of the story of Elmer, a multicoloured elephant who painted himself grey, but who couldn't help but be true to himself. The story tells how Elmer's friends decorated themselves to honour his sense of fun. Many faith celebrations are joyful. They celebrate positive actions and attitudes.

5. If older children are present, reflect that Holi also celebrates the power good has to overcome evil. Retell the legend of Prahlada and Holika using two voices. After each phrase, the children might be invited to hiss or cheer as appropriate!

   Prahlada's father was a king who wanted everybody to worship him. *(Hiss.)*

That was a problem. Prahlada worshipped the Lord Vishnu. He refused to worship the king. *(Cheer.)*

So Prahlada's father tried to kill him. *(Hiss.)*

All his attempts failed. *(Cheer.)*

At last, the king asked the help of his sister, Holika. Holika had been granted a gift. She could touch fire and not be burnt! *(Hiss.)*

Holika invited Prahlada to sit on her lap in the middle of a bonfire. She believed that Prahlada would be burnt to ashes! *(Hiss.)*

Because Holika was using her powers to harm others, the plan failed. She was eaten by the flames and Prahlada walked out of the fire unharmed! *(Cheer.)*

Evil was overcome by good! *(Cheer.)*

6. Explain that, because of this story, bonfires are lit on the night before Holi.

   Conclude by inviting the children to consider how positive attitudes might help to create a bright and happy school and Holi day.

Time for reflection

What colour do you bring to enrich our school community today? Is it the red of a brilliant idea – or the blue of some deep thinking? Do you bring the yellow of laughter or the orange of warm friendship? Who will bring the green of generosity and the purple of passionate care? What will be the picture when our day has ended?

Song

'Together' (*Songs for every Assembly*, Out of the Ark Music)

'Lay my white cloak' (*Come and Praise*, 112)

JANMASHTAMI
Birth of Krishna (August/ September – movable festival)

By Alan M. Barker

Suitable for whole school, particularly new school year

Aim

To focus on the Hindu festival of Janmashtami and the importance of welcome.

Preparation and materials

- **Props** You will need an image of the god Krishna, to organize a group of children to tell the story, and a short piece of flute music for the time of reflection at the end of the assembly.
- To ascertain the date of Janmashtami, visit <www.bbc.co.uk/religion/tools/calendar>.

Pronunciation notes (local pronunciations may vary):

Janmashtami	jan-mash-tamee
Krishna	krish-na
Mandir	man-deer
Bhajans	bar-jans
Kamsa	kam-sa
Devaki	de-va-ki
Vasudeva	va-soo-dee-va

Assembly

1. Reflect that faith communities often celebrate the birth of much-loved prophets and gods. In a festival called Janmashtami, Hindus celebrate Lord Krishna's birthday. The exact date of this celebration varies, but normally falls between August and September.

2. Display the image of Krishna. One meaning of his name is 'dark blue', so he is often depicted with blue skin. Krishna plays the flute – a musical instrument associated with joy, peace and harmony.

3. Explain that it's believed Krishna was born at midnight, so the day before, Hindus in temples (or mandirs) keep a vigil, fast until midnight and sing traditional songs (bhajans). They dance and make offerings. The images of Krishna are bathed in water and milk, dressed in new clothes, placed in cradles and worshipped. Bells are rung. Everyone is glad to welcome Krishna. Favourite foods are offered to Krishna then shared together. The story of Krishna's childhood is also sometimes retold in simple plays.
4. Invite a group of children to retell the story.

The story of Krishna's birth and childhood
Kamsa was an evil and horrible king. He was terribly angry and jealous.

A voice had told him to beware. It said that the eighth child born to his sister would destroy him. Kamsa was so terribly angry and jealous that he decided to imprison his sister Devaki and her husband Vasudeva and, when their children were born, the evil and horrible king had them all killed.

In heaven, Lord Vishnu had seen everything. Eventually, Devaki's eighth child was born. It was a boy – but this was no ordinary baby boy! His name was Krishna. Lord Vishnu had come to save the world from evil. The skies and the earth rejoiced. There was peace and happiness.

The gods helped Vasudeva to slip past the guards. He bravely carried Krishna across the wide Yamuna river to Gokula. A kind cowherd, Nanda, and his wife, Yashoda, welcomed them, and Krishna was left to grow up in their care. He was safe there.

Vasudeva returned to Devaki with the cowherd's baby daughter, but she was a goddess and she was safe too. When King Kamsa tried to kill her, she flew back to the heavens.

As he grew up, Krishna became friends with other boys and girls who looked after the cows. He loved to have fun with them and to play his flute.

Time for reflection

Quietly play the short piece of flute music you have chosen. Invite the children to think about the story and the welcome given to

Krishna. Encourage them to consider all they can do to welcome others at the beginning of the new school year. How does it feel to be a newcomer, perhaps one of the youngest or having just moved here? In what ways can school be made a safe and happy place?

Say one of the following prayers

> *Prayer*
> This is our school.
> Let peace dwell here.
> Let the rooms be full of contentment.
> Let love abide here.
> Love of one another.
> Love of humanity.
> Love of life itself.
> Love of God.
>
> This is our school.
> Let peace dwell here.
> Let the rooms be full of friendship.
> Let love be shared.
> Love of one another.
> Love of all humanity.
> Love of learning.
> Love of life itself.

Songs

'Peace is flowing' (*Come and Praise*, 144)

'Today' (*Songs for Every Assembly*, Out of the Ark Music)

RAKSHA BANDHAN
A festival for brothers and sisters (usually August – movable festival)

By Alan M. Barker

Suitable for whole school

Aim

To reflect on sibling relationships with reference to the Hindu festival of Raksha Bandhan.

Preparation and materials

- **Props** A bracelet (or watch) of sentimental value. Alternatively, the theme could be introduced with some charity wristbands and friendship bracelets. If this assembly is to be held during the last week of the school year, you could include the presentation of friendship bracelets made using the school's colours to give to all leavers. Also, copyright-free images of family celebrations and tying a rakhi from the internet (optional).
- You could ask any children who are Hindus if they would be happy to explain the traditions and significance of this festival and display a rakhi. Alternatively, a rakhi might be purchased locally or online to show when explaining the festival.
- To ascertain the date of Raksha Bandhan, visit <www.bbc.co.uk/religion/tools/calendar>. It is held in the month of Shravana, which means the date is normally in August.

Pronunciation hints (local pronunciations may vary):

Raksha Bandhan	rack-sha ban-dan
Rakhi	rak-i
Shravana	shra-vaa-na
Tilak	ti-lak

Assembly

1. Introduce the assembly by showing the children the bracelet or watch you chose as having sentimental value. Who presented

it? What ties of friendship and kinship does it reflect? Alternatively, display the charity wristbands. Explain their significance – that they are bought and worn to demonstrate support for good causes and campaigns. Also show the friendship bracelets and refer to the practice of making and exchanging them.

2. Go on to refer to the festival of Raksha Bandhan, which is celebrated in Hindu and some Sikh communities across the world. It's a special time when brothers and sisters show love for one another and promise to look after one another.

    If you have been able to gain the agreement of some children who are Hindus to speak about the festival, ask them at this point to describe their experiences of the traditions and ceremonies involved.

3. Sisters tie a colourful bracelet called a rakhi around their brothers' right wrists. They pray that God will keep their brothers safe. They use red powder to make a mark on their brothers' foreheads. This is a sign of blessing, called a tilak. In return, brothers promise to look after their sisters during the coming year. They give their sisters a gift of money or jewellery. Sweets are also shared.

4. The word 'Raksha' means 'protection' and 'Bandhan' means 'to tie'. So Raksha Bandhan is a festival that strengthens family ties. Many women send rakhis to any of their brothers who live far away. Also, cousins and friends ensure that those who don't have brothers or sisters are not left out!

5. Refer to the forthcoming school holidays and how the children will be spending time together at home. Acknowledge that this isn't always easy. Sometimes brothers and sisters argue or become jealous of one another. In family life, we have to learn understanding and patience. Invite the children to reflect how they will care for one another during the holidays. What might they do to keep one another safe? Reflect on the importance of road safety and avoiding hazardous play areas.

6. Alternatively, observe that some of the children will know how difficult it is to be parted from brothers and sisters. Invite the children to affirm their family ties with phrases such as, 'I appreciate my brother because . . .', 'I care about my sister because . . .'. Such contributions might be prepared beforehand or arise spontaneously. Refer to those who will

soon be moving to new schools. The support and prayers of brothers, sisters and friends can mean so much. Presentations of friendship bracelets or other leaving gifts might be made at this point in the assembly.

7. Conclude with the thought that, whatever our faith, Raksha Bandhan shows how belief in God and concern for one another can bind us together and make us strong.

Time for reflection

Be thankful for family ties. Pray for God's blessing and protection on those who are close to you.

Songs

'Together' (*Songs for Every Assembly*, Out of the Ark Music)

'The family of man' (*Come and Praise*, 69)

VASANT PANCHAMI
A new beginning (January/ February – movable festival)

By Alan M. Barker

Suitable for whole school

Aim

To celebrate new beginnings in life and learning.

Preparation and materials

- This assembly could either be timed to coincide with Vasant Panchami or, alternatively, held later in March.
- **Props** Some vases of daffodils, to provide a point of focus – ideally some in bud and others that some warmth has coaxed into more open flowers, an overhead projector or flipchart on which to compile a springtime alphabet.
- Ascertain the date of Vasant Panchami by visiting <www.bbc.co.uk/religion/tools/calendar>.

Pronunciation notes (local pronunciations may vary):

| Vasant Panchami | va-sant pan-chaa-me |
| Saraswati | sara-swat-ee ('swat' rhymes with 'cat') |

Assembly

1. Reflect that, for many in the northern hemisphere, spring begins on 21 March. In India, however, many Hindus mark the first day of spring with the festival of Vasant Panchami, which is held between late January and mid-February. People dress in yellow to celebrate new life, offer yellow flowers to each other and the gods and goddesses and cook a special dish using saffron, which turns it yellow.

2. The festival is dedicated to Saraswati, goddess of learning and wisdom. It's thus the tradition that, at this time, young children begin to learn how to write the alphabet. Hindus believe that doing so at this time will bring the children blessing and wisdom.

Invite the children to reflect on new beginnings. When and how did they learn the alphabet? Do they recall their first day at school? How has their knowledge and understanding grown?

3. Challenge everyone with the task of creating an alphabet, associating each letter with springtime sights and feelings. Explain that the task isn't easy. Everyone's help will be needed. Refer to the vases of daffodils, saying that we learn together and are brightest in a bunch. Just as the warmth of the sun causes buds to flower, it's encouragement that brings out the best in us.

4. Start with the letters A to E. In your springtime alphabet:
   - A might be for awake and alive
   - B is for buds, busy bees and brilliant butterflies
   - C is for cheerful crocuses and colourful changes
   - D is for dancing daffodils and delight
   - E for energy, eggs and excitement.

5. Point out that some of the words also describe positive approaches to learning. Will the children be 'awake and alive' to new ideas? How 'busy, brilliant and cheerful' will they be in making new beginnings?

6. Refer again to the vases of daffodils. By the end of school, more buds will have opened into flowers. Express the hope that the day will also bring out the best in each and every student too!

7. Place the daffodils somewhere the children can see them, so that they can watch them opening and be reminded of this thought.

Time for reflection

Spend a little time reflecting on new beginnings and how we can improve.

Prayer
Just as the warmth of the sun opens leaves and buds, so may being together today open our hearts and minds to learn.
Amen

Songs

'Living and learning' (*Songs for Every Assembly*, Out of the Ark Music)

'It's a new day' (*Come and Praise*, 106)

5
ISLAM

AL-HIJRAH
Muhammad's migration from Mecca to Medina, Islamic New Year (varies – movable festival)

By Janice Ross

Suitable for Key Stage 2

Aim

To consider the meaning of community and the beginnings of Islam.

Preparation and materials

- **Props** The word 'community' written on a whiteboard (leaving space to add 'communitas' later, during the assembly), map of Saudi Arabia and school badge.
- To ascertain the date of Al-Hijrah, visit <www.bbc.co.uk/religion/tools/calendar>.

Assembly

1. Explain that today in assembly you are going to be thinking about the meaning of the word 'community'. Ask the children to suggest what is meant when we talk of 'the community'.

2. Show the school badge. The school is also a community. A community is also a group of people of all ages brought together with a common goal. In the case of the school, that goal is education and learning how to live together and belong. Mention could also be made of the school's ethos.

3. Even within the school there are further communities of different types. Ask for a show of hands for children who belong to each of the following. Ask, 'Do we have a community of sportspeople in the school? Do we have a community of music lovers in the school? Do we have a community of book lovers in the school?' and so on. 'Community' here means people brought together by a

common interest. It is good to have friends who enjoy the same things that we do. (If yours is a community school, it would be useful to consider all the clubs that use its facilities.)

4. The word 'community' is derived from a Latin word 'communitas' (meaning 'fellowship'), from 'communis' (meaning 'common', 'general' or 'universal'). Write this on the whiteboard.

5. Tell the following story.

How Islam began

Many years ago, there was a large community called Mecca. It is still there today. *(Locate Mecca on the map of Saudi Arabia. If time permits, identify the physical geography of the country.)* Hundreds of years ago, Mecca was a very holy city to many tribes of Arab people. The people of Mecca and Saudi Arabia had many things in common. The land was largely poor and barren. The climate was very hot and there was a scarcity of water. Yet they were made up of lots of different clans and religions. They worshipped a supreme god, but many idols as well. A lot of quarrelling and bickering went on between the tribes over everything from camels to gods.

A young man named Muhammad lived in Mecca with his uncle. Muhammad was a special young man who spent many hours on his own, meditating and seeking to know God and truth. He wanted to bring unity to the tribes, he wanted to bring a sense of community. He believed that there was only one God and he went around speaking about this. Because of his interest in spiritual things, he was called a prophet, which means someone who hears from God. The prophet Muhammad soon had a number of followers – people from many different tribes, who lived together and shared everything they had – but he also had many enemies who liked things just the way they had always been.

So it came about that Muhammad and his friends had to flee from Mecca and move north to a place called Medina. *(Locate Medina on the map of Saudi Arabia.)*

There they found the people more willing to listen. The people of Medina believed that the teachings of the prophet

Muhammad were the right way to live, and many joined his community.

A number of years later, Muhammad went back to Mecca, now with a huge number of followers called Muslims, and, over the years, the people in Mecca became Muslims too. 'Muslim' is the name for people who believe that Muhammad was Allah's (God's) last prophet and who read the holy book of the Islamic faith called the Qur'an. As a result, Mecca is still a very important place that thousands of Muslims visit each year.

6. Today, there are more than a billion Muslims in the world. They still come from many different tribes, but the Islamic faith has brought many of them a great sense of unity.

7. Al-Hijrah celebrates the day the prophet Muhammad left Mecca to travel to Medina in AD 622 as this led to the establishment of the Muslim community there. Thus, Muslim years are dated from this time and are termed 'AH', which stands for 'after the Hijrah', so Al-Hijrah is the beginning of the Islamic New Year. Muslims, however, don't celebrate it in as lively a way as New Year's Eve or 1 January is celebrated in the UK. It is a much quieter affair. Stories are told in mosques of the prophet and his companions and Muslims think about how they can move from bad ways of living to live in better ways.

8. So now we have learnt that the word 'community' can also refer to a group of millions of people all over the world who share a common faith.

Time for reflection

What do you appreciate about your community? Which faith communities do you have in your school? Think about your class, your school, any club you are part of, your town or surrounding area and your faith group, if appropriate.

It is a gift to have friends who come together with you to share their hobbies and interests, their education, their lives and their faith.

Prayer
Thank you for our school community – for our friends and teachers, our clubs and our shared desire to learn. Thank you

for our wider community – our neighbours, our shopkeepers, for places like the library, the shops, the local hospital, services that we all share. Thank you for our faith – for the things that we believe in about God and for all who seek to teach us about these important issues.
Amen

♪ Song

'The family of man' (*Come and Praise*, 69)

EID UL-ADHA
Festival of sacrifice
(varies – movable festival)

By Jude Scrutton

Suitable for Key Stages 1 and 2

Aim

To explore the festival of Eid ul-Adha.

Preparation and materials

- **Props** Pictures of different phases of the moon in the course of a year, showing how it changes shape from a fine crescent to a full moon (type 'moon shape diary' into any search engine on the internet), ensuring that you have a picture of what it looks like on the correct date for Eid ul-Adha in the current year, and an Eid greetings card. A candle and means to light it.
- To ascertain the date of Eid ul-Adha, visit <www.bbc.co.uk/religion/tools/calendar>.

Assembly

1. Look at what shape the moon is on the correct date for Eid ul-Adha this year. Explain that many people look at the crescent shape of the moon around this time when they are celebrating a very important religious festival. Ask the children if they know what the festival is. Give clues as to what faith the festival relates to by asking questions such as 'Do you think we talk about the crescent moon at Christmas time?' or 'Do you know of any festivals that move through the year with phases of the moon?' (Easter, Passover, most of the Muslim festivals. . .)

2. Introduce the festival of Eid ul-Adha. Tell the children that Adha ('festival of sacrifice'), also known as the Greater Eid, is the second most important festival in the Muslim calendar.

3. Explain that the festival recalls how the prophet Ibrahim (whom Jews and Christians call 'Abraham') was willing to sacrifice his

son Ishmael (rather than Isaac, as the story has it in the Bible) when God ordered him to do the following.

Allah (God) appeared to Ibrahim in a dream and asked him to sacrifice his son Ishmael as an act of obedience to Allah. The devil tempted Ibrahim by saying that he should disobey Allah and spare his son. As Ibrahim was about to kill his son, Allah stopped him and gave him a lamb to sacrifice instead.

4. Eid ul-Adha is a public holiday in Muslim countries. Explain that Muslims all over the world who can afford it sacrifice a sheep (sometimes a goat) as a reminder of Ibrahim's obedience to Allah. (Explain that, in Britain, the law is that these animals can only be killed at a licensed slaughterhouse.)

The meat is shared out equally among family, friends, neighbours and the poor.

Eid usually starts with Muslims going to the mosque for prayers at daybreak, dressed in their best clothes, and thanking Allah for all the blessings they have received.

5. At Eid, it is obligatory to give a set amount of money to charity, to be used to help poor people to buy new clothes and food so that they too can celebrate.

Time for reflection

(Light a candle and ask the children to reflect on the festival of Eid.)

God, Allah, expects us all to share what we have. How could you share some of the good things that you have today?

> *Prayer*
> Help us to learn about all faiths and be tolerant and understanding of different people's beliefs.
> May we be generous with all that we have, sharing our things and giving our friendship.
> **Amen**

Song

'Lord of the dance' (*Come and Praise*, 22)

EID UL-FITR
End of Ramadan
(varies – movable festival)

By Janice Ross

Suitable for Key Stage 2

Aim

To consider the meaning of the words Eid ul-Fitr and understand the different facets of the festival.

Preparation and materials

- **Background** This is a Muslim holiday marking the end of Ramadan, the holy month of fasting. The festival of Eid ul-Fitr begins with the sighting of the new moon and lasts for two days. 'Eid' is from an Arabic word 'Id', meaning 'feast'. 'Fitr' means 'breaking the fast'. 'Eid Mubarak' means 'blessed Eid' and is the usual greeting on these days.
- **Props** Items linked to celebrations (such as holly, crackers, fireworks, horseshoe, anniversary card, candles, single rose, jelly, Christmas pudding), a whiteboard or noticeboard to put up the phrases 'Eid = festivity', 'Fitr = breaking the fast', 'Eid Mubarak = blessed Eid', items linked to Eid – a packet of dates, an Eid greetings card or a copyright-free image of the festival from the internet. You will also need to write or project the following sentences on a whiteboard (if you have any Muslim children who would be happy to help with this exercise in the assembly, it helps a great deal):

They pray to God, Allah.
They clean their teeth.
They take a shower.
They put on new or at least their best clothes and perfume.
They say a special Eid prayer.
They have a small breakfast, often with dates.
They go to the mosque for special morning prayers.
They greet family and friends and share a meal together.

These sentences are shown here in the correct order. Mix them up on the board; you will ask the children to put them in the right order.

Finally, a small piece of paper for each child and member of staff and enough dates for the children to have one each as they leave the assembly (optional, and take care regarding any allergies and mention that they have stones).

- Ascertain the date of Eid ul-Fitr by visiting <www.bbc.co.uk/religion/tools/calendar>.

Pronunciation notes (local pronunciations may vary):

Eid ul-Fitr   eed ul-fit-r
Mubarak   moo-ba-rack

Assembly

1. All people everywhere love a celebration. They may celebrate on different days, in different ways, but usually a celebration means joy and happiness.

2. Play the game 'Guess the celebration' by showing some of the items suggested above as being linked to celebrations, and see if the children guess correctly. Alternatively, identify and discuss briefly when we celebrate, how we do so and with whom. Which celebration is the biggest you have been involved in?

3. Explain that Muslims all over the world hold a special celebration called Eid ul-Fitr once a year. This doesn't happen on the same day each year because Muslim festivals depend on the moon for their date, but this year it starts on *(fill in date)* and, as always, lasts two days.

4. On the whiteboard, point out the following words and their meanings that you prepared: 'Eid = festivity', 'Fitr = breaking the fast', 'Eid Mubarak = blessed Eid'. When Muslims meet each other during the festival they greet each other with the words 'Eid Mubarak', a bit like we say 'Happy Christmas'.

5. Consider the words and phrases one at a time and ask the children to suggest what kind of celebrating might be involved. So, for example, 'Eid' suggests fun, laughter, decorations (show the Eid greetings card), 'Fitr' links this festival to Ramadan and suggests there may be food involved (show the packet of dates) and 'Mubarak' suggests it is to do with religion and faith.

6. The first thing that happens on Eid ul-Fitr is that the many Muslims all over the world wake up before sunrise, as they have been doing for the past 30 days, then they all prepare for the festival in the very same way! Write or project the following sentences about these preparations, in a random order, on the whiteboard for the children to put in the correct sequence. (They can call out the sentences; when they get them in the right order, put a number beside each sentence to show where it is in the correct sequence.) If, as mentioned above, you have some Muslim children in your school and they have agreed to help you with this exercise beforehand, ask them to come to the board at this point. Once the exercise is completed, display the sentences in the correct order:

They pray to God, Allah.
They clean their teeth.
They take a shower.
They put on new or at least their best clothes and perfume.
They say a special Eid prayer.
They have a small breakfast, often with dates.
They go to the mosque for special morning prayers.
They greet family and friends and share a meal together.

7. Eid ul-Fitr is very much a community celebration, so a lot of visiting takes place over these two days, including to the graves of relatives. There is a lot of eating, giving of presents, wearing new clothes and general fun and laughter. At Eid ul-Fitr, Muslims are not only celebrating the end of fasting but also thanking Allah for the help and strength he gave them throughout the previous month of Ramadan while they were fasting to help them practise self-control.

8. During Ramadan, Muslims consider the kinds of lives they have been living. Have they shown kindness and thoughtfulness to others in their family and in the wider community? Have they been forgiving when someone has wronged them? These are all things that their holy book, the Qur'an, tells them to practise.

9. So with the happy festival of Eid ul-Fitr comes a time to say sorry to one another, to make amends. People are encouraged to forgive and forget any differences or past grievances they have had during the year. This is another reason why Eid ul-Fitr is a time of such great joy in the Muslim community – it is a fresh start.

Time for reflection

Perhaps we could use this time to think about anger or grudges we might be holding towards someone we know. We are going to use the small pieces of paper that you have all been given to help with this (make sure the staff each get one too). Each of us is to think about someone we need to forgive. It might be a family member, a friend, an adult. Imagine writing (but don't actually write) what has angered or hurt you on this paper. If and when you are ready to forgive, screw up the paper and drop it in the bin as you leave the hall. Now you will be able to go away with a happier heart.

The children could be offered a date *(once again, tell them not to eat the stones and check about any allergies)* as they leave the assembly. Some will not have tasted this fruit before, but it is traditionally eaten during Eid ul-Fitr.

> *Prayer*
> Thank you for celebrations, for happy times that we spend with people we love. Bless those who are enjoying the end of a time of fasting. May the lessons they have learnt bring them happiness, forgiveness and a sense of community.
> **Amen**

Song

'Give us hope, Lord' (*Come and Praise*, 87)

RAMADAN
Month-long fast
(varies – movable festival)

By Janice Ross

Suitable for Key Stage 2

Aim

To consider how denying ourselves something we crave teaches us self-control and makes us grateful for those things we take for granted.

Preparation and materials

- **Background** The Muslim year is based on a lunar calendar. Ramadan occurs in the ninth month of the lunar calendar. It is a movable festival, as it is dependent on the phases of the moon, and moves forward by 10 or 11 days each year. The festival begins with the sighting of a new moon and lasts for a month. Ramadan is a time of self-examination and increasing religious devotion, during which Muslims fast from sunrise to sunset. The purpose of this is to bring their physical needs into submission to the spiritual, to stay away from worldly desires and focus on Allah (God) and his blessings. Muslims believe that when they deny themselves food, they are actually learning lessons in humility, self-control and empathy.
- **Props** There are lots of videos on the internet that you could use to help children get the 'feel' of Ramadan. Check for copyright issues and that they conform to your school's rules. You will also need a plate of a chocolatey tray-bake or cake, cut into pieces, some slightly smaller and some notably larger than others. Check regarding allergies. Finally, you will need a teaching clock.
- To ascertain the date Ramadan starts, visit <www.bbc.co.uk/religion/tools/calendar>.

Pronunciation notes:

    Suhoor   soo-hor
    Iftar   if-tar

Assembly

1. Invite some children from a variety of classes to come and share the tray-bake or cake. Observe the tussle for the biggest bits!

2. Ask the children if they had difficulty choosing which piece to have. Who went for the biggest? Who thought, just for a second, about not being greedy and taking a small piece? Not easy when it is such a lovely tray-bake/cake, is it?!

3. Explain that no one finds it easy to say 'No!' to the little voice inside us suggesting that we should get the biggest or best or be served first. This is called selfishness and is something we are all prone to, something in the human character.

4. Explain that if there were some Muslim children about 12 years old or older and adults who came to our assembly and it took place during Ramadan, they would not even have come forward for the smallest piece of cake, even if they loved it. That is because they would be keeping the fast of Ramadan. During Ramadan, which lasts for one month, no food is eaten during daylight hours. Thousands of Muslims all over the world take part in this fast. Muslims go to school and work as usual during Ramadan, but more time is spent praying, reading their holy book, the Qur'an, and being charitable to the poor. Before the sun rises in the morning, when it is still dark, everyone is woken up and has a small breakfast, called suhoor. This has to last them right through the day until the sun sets and it is dark again. Then, once again, they are allowed to eat some food, this time called iftar.

5. Explain that although children don't have to fast as older children and adults do because Islam recognizes that their bodies need a steady supply of energy, lots of children of their age join in with the Ramadan fast by eating less sweet food or giving some of their pocket money to charity. They may fast for part of the day or at the weekend, when they can take life a bit more slowly – it's up to them and their families to decide.

6. Bring out the teaching clock and use it to show when day breaks at this time of year and when darkness falls. Ask the children, 'How many hours of daylight do we have? Would this discipline of fasting be difficult for you? Would it be more difficult in a hot country, a cold country?' Identify times during the day when it might be particularly difficult to fast –

breaktime, lunchtime, when they come home after school. Think about any mouthwatering aromas coming from the school kitchen.

7. Some children could be asked to complete this sentence:
   'If I smelled . . . my tummy would rumble!'

8. Ask the children to suggest what might be learnt from a month of denying ourselves food whenever we felt like having it. Here are some examples of possible answers they might give.
   - We learn to say 'No' to ourselves and all the cravings of our bodies.
   - We learn what it feels like to be weak and need strength from a different source.
   - We learn to identify with the many poor in the world who live like this most days.
   - We learn to focus on God and his blessings.
   - We learn that to wait for things is actually good for us.

9. At the end of Ramadan comes Eid ul-Fitr, a huge festival. Ask the children, 'What do you think Muslims do during this festival?' The answer is, they go to pray at their local mosque and have lots to eat!

Time for reflection

Saying 'No' to what we want is often difficult. No one likes to deny themselves food, TV, long lie-ins at the weekend. When do you find it hard to say 'No'?

Prayer
We thank you for all that we have to eat. Please be with those who are fasting at this time, that they might feel closer to you as a result of this discipline.
Amen

Song

'Give us hope, Lord' (*Come and Praise*, 87)

6
JAINISM

MAHAVIRA JAYANTI
Mahavira's birthday
(March/April – movable festival)

By Rebecca Parkinson

Suitable for whole school

Aim

To understand the Jain festival of Mahavira Jayanti.

Preparation and materials

- **Props** Brightly coloured flags – these could simply be sticks with any colour of rectangle attached or could be in the form of bunting. Also, some milk, rice, fruit, perfume or incense, lamp and water – for the children to hold.

Pronunciation notes (local pronunciations may vary):

Mahavira Jayanti	ma-have-era jay-anti
Vardhamana	var-daa-manna
Devananda	dev-a-nanda
Tirthankaras	ter-than-kaa-ras

Assembly

1. Ask the children if they can think of any special things they do to celebrate a particular occasion. You may need to guide them to think about Christmas, Easter, Eid, Hanukkah, Diwali and other festivals. Explain that you are going to tell them about another special festival called Mahavira Jayanti, which is particularly celebrated in India, but is becoming more popular in other parts of the world.

2. Say that, before you tell them about the festival, you are going to tell them about the man who was a religious teacher and a key figure in shaping a religion called Jainism, its followers being called Jains.

3. **The story of Mahavira**

    About 2,500 years ago, a prince called Vardhamana was born in India. He was the son of King Siddhartha and Queen Devananda (or Trishala, Videhadinna or Priyakarini in other traditions). Vardhamana grew up in the royal palace, but when he was about 30 years old, following the death of both of his parents, he decided to leave the luxury of palace life and, instead, spend his time fasting and meditating. For the next 12½ years, Vardhamana went without food for long periods of time. He often had no clothes to wear and nowhere to sleep.

    Through these experiences Jains believe that Vardhamana became 'enlightened'. 'Enlightened' means that someone has attained so much special spiritual knowledge that they can eventually understand everything and become perfect. Jains call people who become enlightened 'Tirthankaras'. In the Jain religion there are 24 Tirthankaras, and Vardhamana was the last of these in our time. When Vardhamana became enlightened, he came to be known as Mahavira.

    Once Mahavira became enlightened, he began to teach what he had learnt and follow a very old way of life. He was not a founder of a religion; rather, he built on what other people had discovered before him. When he died (at the age of 72), he had a following of about 14,000 monks and 36,000 nuns.

4. Jains have five main beliefs.

    - No violence and respect for living things. All Jains are vegetarians and a few are so determined to not kill any animal that they sweep the path ahead of them before they walk to ensure that they don't step on any insects. Some very devoted Jains even wear masks so that they don't accidentally breathe in an insect and thus kill it. Jains also believe that you should not hurt the feelings of another living being.
    - You should not lie, but always tell the truth.
    - You should never steal or cheat.
    - Husbands and wives should always stay together.
    - You should not seek material things, such as food, riches, fashionable clothes.

5. Ask for volunteers to come to the front and hold the flags. Explain that the date for the festival of Mahavira Jayanti celebrated by Jains changes, but is usually in March or April.

It is the most important festival for Jains and celebrates Mahavira's birthday. Shrines and temples are decorated with flags and everyone dresses in bright clothes to take part in a procession. Before the procession begins, an idol of Mahavira is given a ritual bath and then placed in a cradle so it can be carried through the streets. Celebrations continue late into the night.

6. During Mahavira Jayanti, people often give gifts to the poor. Explain that you want the children to guess what gifts are usually given by listening to the sets of clues below. Read one clue, then let a child make a guess, then read a second clue and let a different child guess and so on until a child guesses correctly.

First object
- This gift is white.
- It is a drink.
- It comes from a cow.

The answer is milk. Ask a child to come out and hold the milk.

Second object
- In this country we eat a wide variety of food, but in some countries, this is almost all they eat.
- It is made up of tiny grains.
- You cook it with boiling water.
- You often have it with curry or chilli.

The answer is rice. Ask a child to come up and hold the rice.

Third object
- This helps keep you healthy.
- They can be red, green, yellow, purple – in fact, all sorts of colours!
- Some are long and thin, some are small and round, most are juicy.
- You can buy them at lots of food shops and supermarkets.

The answer is fruit. Ask a child to come up and hold the fruit.

Fourth object
- People buy it as a present, but it can be very expensive.
- It smells nice.
- Usually you squirt it *(for perfume)*/burn it *(for incense)*.

The answer is perfume/incense. Ask a child to come up and hold the perfume/incense.

Fifth object
- These brighten up a dark room.

- Now, we switch them on, but years ago, they could have used gas, oil or wax.
- They have bulbs in them.

The answer is lamp. Ask a child to come up and hold the lamp.

Sixth object
- It is made up of hydrogen and oxygen.
- You cannot survive without it.
- About 70 per cent of your body is made up of this.
- It is wet.

The answer is water. Ask a child to come out and hold the water.

7. Today, as well as millions of Jains living in India, there are many thousands in other parts of the world. The festival of Mahavira Jayanti is a bright, noisy, happy festival, during which Jains celebrate the birthday and life of Mahavira. Its true meaning, however, is that it helps the Jain community to continue to respect all living things and live in peace. Those are great lessons for us all to learn.

Time for reflection

During Mahavira Jayanti, many people text their friends and families, just as many of us do on special occasions. Here are two of the texts that it proved popular to send in 2011. Ask the children to think about what the words mean as you read them slowly:

May Lord Mahavira bless you abundantly and fill your life with the virtue of truth, non-violence and compassion. Happy Mahavira Jayanti.

Little keys can open big locks. Simple words can express great thoughts. I hope my simple prayer can make your life great. Happy Mahavira Jayanti.

Prayer
Please help us always to respect living things, whether they are plants, animals or other humans.
Thank you for the beauty of your creation. Please help us always to look after your world.
Amen

Song

'All things bright and beautiful' (*Come and Praise*, 3)

PARYUSANA
A time to pray and learn (August/September – movable festival)

By Rebecca Parkinson

Suitable for whole school

Aim

To understand the Jain festival of Paryusana.

Preparation and materials

- **Props** Objects that indicate a certain type of weather – sunglasses for sunshine, an umbrella for rain, a hat and scarf for cold, a sledge for snow, a bucket and spade for sunny, a windmill for windy, wellies for snow or rain and so on. Also, write the school motto on a large piece of paper.

Pronunciation notes (local pronunciations may vary):

    Paryusana   pa-ree-oo-sana

Assembly

1. In turn, hold up each of the objects listed as props above and ask the children to suggest what sort of weather they would use them in. Also, each time, ask a child to come to the front to hold that item by their side.

2. Explain that you are going to play a game where you will say different weather types and, as you say them, the children holding the props are to make the appropriate action for their prop. For example, if you were to say 'summer', one child would put the sunglasses on and another child would pretend to dig in the sand and fill up the bucket. If you were to say 'snow', one child would pull on the wellies while another would pretend to sledge. If you were to say 'rain', one child would put up the umbrella and another would put on the wellies. If you were to say 'windy', one child would blow on the windmill to make the sails go round.

3. Say the weather words in different orders so that the children have to make their responses quickly. Ask all the other children to do the actions at the same time as those at the front. You may like to ask another child to call out the weather words instead of you.

4. Ask the children if any of them have heard of the 'rainy season'. Explain that whereas in this country it can rain at any time of the year, in some parts of the world they have heavy rainfall for a few months while the rest of the year it is completely dry. Ask if the children can think of any problems that a 'rainy season' could cause. Usual suggestions are flooding, houses being washed away, crops destroyed and, in the dry season, drought and famine.

The Jain religion, which is mainly followed in India although Jains can now be found in most other countries of the world, has turned the rainy season into a positive time. In India, holy men and women spend most of their time travelling from place to place, but during the rainy season it is not possible to do this, so they settle in a village or town for a few months. This means that they are available to instruct and guide the people who live there during this time.

It is in the middle of the rainy season that Jains celebrate the festival of Paryusana. The festival lasts eight days and Jains will visit the temples and shrines regularly to be taught by the holy men and women and make confessions. Jains also often spend time fasting and meditating.

5. Most festivals tend to be noisy, colourful events. The festival of Paryusana is not like that – it is about looking inwardly at ourselves and finding inner peace. At the end of the eight days, Jains hope that their time of reflection and teaching will have purified them, so that they are less bothered about material things (such as money, cars, clothes, food) and, as a result, happier than they were previously.

6. Ask the children if they know what a 'motto' is. If you have a school motto, show the piece of paper you prepared previously and make particular reference to this. If not, go straight to the next step.

The Jains have a motto: 'Live and let live'. Ask the children what they think this means. Explain that the festival of Paryusana aims to help Jains live their own lives so that they enjoy them fully, but it also aims to remind them that they must not judge other people and must treat everybody with respect, as if they were of great importance. Jains hope that, following the festival of Paryusana, they will try to make other people happy rather than just pleasing themselves. That is a good thing for all of us to aim to do.

Time for reflection

Think about the Jain motto: 'Live and let live'. How do we treat other people? Are we kind to some and unkind to others? Do we treat rich or famous people differently from the way we treat someone who is poor or unpopular?

There may be people in school who are different and whom we find difficult to like. Spend a few minutes realizing that they too are special, and try to think of a way in which you could make them happy today.

Prayer
(The verse below is learnt by heart and recited during the festival of Paryusana. Below it, it appears again, but the words have been changed slightly so that they are in the form of a prayer.)

I grant forgiveness to all living beings.
May all living beings grant me forgiveness.
My friendship is with all living beings.
My enmity is totally non-existent.
Let there be peace, harmony and prosperity for all.

Please help me always to forgive.
I am sorry for the times that I have treated any living thing wrongly.
Please help me to treat living things well and with respect.
Help me to be at peace with all things.
Please let everyone learn to live in peace and harmony, for the sake of a better world.
Amen

Song

'One more step' (*Come and Praise*, 47)

7
JUDAISM

ROSH HASHANAH
Jewish New Year, Day of Remembrance, Day of Judgement (September/October – movable festival)

By Manon Ceridwen Parry

Suitable for whole school

Aim

To learn about the Jewish festival of Rosh Hashanah and think about how different sounds make us feel different things.

Preparation and materials

- **Background** Rosh Hashanah (literally, 'head of the year') is the celebration of the Jewish New Year, also called the Day of Remembrance as it traditionally commemorates the creation of the world. It is also called the Day of Judgement when God judges the balance between the good and bad deeds during the year, and it marks the start of ten days of self-examination and penitence, at the end of which is Yom Kippur. The date is movable and is on the first (sometimes second) day of Tishri, which is in September or October.
- **Props** Apples and a jar of honey. Also, if you can, locate a shofar at your local RE centre or else find some pictures of one in books or on the internet. A shofar is an instrument made from the horn of a kosher animal, usually a ram but it can be from a sheep or goat, that is blown during services in the synagogue on Rosh Hashanah as it is the Jewish New Year. In ancient times, it was used to announce the new moon. Finally, find sources of a couple of contrasting sounds – lively and still music or a triangle and a drum or a siren and a baby's cry, for example – plus a piece of calming music to play at the end of assembly. Note that MP3 players and smartphones may also have applications with different evocative sounds or noises that you could use.

Pronunciation notes (local pronunciations may vary):

Rosh Hashanah	rosh huh-shanna
shofar	show-fa (like 'sofa')
Yom Kippur	yom ki-poor

Assembly

1. Discuss the New Year traditions the children keep – traditions that are part of their culture or family traditions. Do they, for example, make New Year's resolutions? Do they or their families have New Year's Eve parties? Are there any other different traditions? Maybe they sing special songs, such as 'Auld Lang Syne', count down the seconds to midnight and so on.

2. Explain that the Jewish festival of New Year happens in September or October, not January, lasts two days and is the start of the ten days leading to Yom Kippur, the Day of Atonement. It is a special time for Jews and Yom Kippur is the most special of the Jewish festivals, so a lot of preparation is required.

3. On Rosh Hashanah, the Jewish New Year, Jews believe that God looks at each person to see what they have done, good or bad, in the last year. They then have ten days to 'repent' the bad (literally turn around) and be good. On Yom Kippur, if they have tried hard to be good and made friends with people they've argued with, they will be forgiven.

4. As well as special stories, there are also special practices. Apples and honey are eaten on Rosh Hashanah because, for the coming year, they want sweetness and happiness in their lives and wish it for other people by giving them these sweet things.

5. Show the children the shofar or pictures of one and tell them about it. Tell them that a shofar is an instrument made from the horn of a kosher animal, usually a ram, but it can be from a sheep or goat, that is blown in services in the synagogue on Rosh Hashanah as it is the Jewish New Year. In ancient times, it was used to announce a new moon or the arrival of a king. It has a special sound and is supposed to remind everyone about God and call them back to him, reminiscent of Moses on Mount Sinai. Just as people prepare for a visit by a king, so people need to ensure that they are ready for God, who will 'judge' their behaviour – that is, decide if they have been

good or bad. Jewish people who are used to this sound will associate it with New Year and with this process of judgement – weighing up how good or bad someone has been.

6. Other things have their own special sounds too, and remind us of different things. Depending on what you have brought, discuss with the children how different sounds make them feel – a drumbeat makes us want to dance, dreamy music or sounds make us want to sleep, a baby's cry makes us feel anxious, a siren makes us feel worried that someone's been hurt and so on. Any evocative sounds will do – the idea is to discuss how sounds make us feel different things. Remind the children that the sound the shofar makes reminds Jewish people of the need to turn to God and be sorry for the wrong things they may have done.

Time for reflection

Play the calming music you chose. Say that it helps us reflect, be calm and still and think. Encourage the children to use the next few minutes to think about anything they may have done that is wrong and how they will change.

Prayer
Help us to respect others and respect ourselves.
Help us to care for others and care for ourselves.
Help us to be sorry when we hurt others and try to put things right.
May this New Year be filled with sweetness,
For ourselves, our friends and families.
Amen

Song

'Kum ba yah' (*Come and Praise*, 68)

YOM KIPPUR
Day of Atonement (September/October – movable festival)

By Manon Ceridwen Parry

Suitable for whole school

Aims

To learn about the festival of Yom Kippur and think about its themes of wrongdoing and forgiveness.

Preparation and materials

- **Background** Yom Kippur is the most solemn and sacred day of the Jewish year. It is held on the tenth day after Rosh Hashanah and marks the anniversary of Moses' return from Mount Sinai with the second set of the Ten Commandments. During this ten-day period, the aim is to make amends for what God found at Rosh Hashanah, the Jewish New Year, the Day of Judgement. On Yom Kippur, the Day of Atonement, adults and older children fast (abstain from all food and drink), observe other rituals and attend five services in the synagogue. By the end of the day, they are forgiven. Even Jews who are not especially religious tend to observe Yom Kippur.
- **Props** Think about the school's practices regarding encouraging good behaviour so that you can incorporate them into the assembly. In the assembly that follows, the 'Good Book' method is referred to, but this can be altered to reflect your school's practices if required. If your school does employ a Good Book, either ensure that you have it with you during the assembly or make one to show. This could simply be a notebook with 'Good Book' written or typed on a label in large letters and stuck on the cover. Also, find a recording of some typical Jewish folk music and learn a simple traditional circle dance to teach the children (optional).

Pronunciation notes (local pronunciations may vary):

Yom Kippur	yom ki-poor
Rosh Hashanah	rosh huh-shanna

Assembly

1. Talk about the different ways in which schools encourage good behaviour – traffic lights, with red and yellow cards being given to those who misbehave, for example. Ask the children to tell you about ways in which their clubs, societies and homes encourage good behaviour.

2. Talk about the 'Good Book' method. In some schools, any member of a school – teachers and pupils – can write the names of anyone who is being really good, working hard or showing real care and concern for others in the Good Book.

3. Refer the children back to Rosh Hashanah, especially if it has been the subject of a previous assembly. Explain how, ten days before Yom Kippur, Rosh Hashanah is celebrated as the Jewish New Year. On that day, traditionally, God judges their behaviour over the past year and then, for the ten days that follow, Jews try to make amends by being good, making friends with people they've fallen out with and so on.

    Yom Kippur is the special festival at the end of those ten days when Jews think especially about what they've done wrong and ask God for his forgiveness. They do this at home and at special services (five altogether) in the synagogue.

4. To help them concentrate on their prayers, adults and older children (though not younger children, babies, older people and those who are ill) fast, which means that they don't eat or drink anything on Yom Kippur.

5. Explain that the reason you have brought the Good Book with you is that it is a similar idea to a special book that appears in stories about Yom Kippur. It is called 'The Book of Life', and Jews believe that this is where God writes down all the good and bad things a person has done in the past year. On Rosh Hashanah, Jewish New Year's Day, God makes a judgement about how the good and the bad balance out. So it is a bit like the Good Book, but with one big difference – only especially good things are written in the Good Book.

6. At the end of Yom Kippur, the Book of Life is closed and sealed according to Jewish tradition, and God makes a decision about what the New Year will be like for a person, based on how he or she has been in the past year.

7. To celebrate the end of Yom Kippur and God's forgiveness, Jews break their fast by having a special party.

Time for reflection

(Open your Good Book and ask the children to sit quietly and reflectively.)

What would you like to be written about you in the Good Book? Maybe you would like to think about any wrong things you have done and how you might put them right.

> *Prayer*
> Help us to be kind, respectful and loving in all that we think, do and say.
> Help us to be sorry when we hurt others and to try to put things right.
> **Amen**

*(**Note:** You may like to use the prayer at the end of the previous assembly about Rosh Hashanah, if you have held that assembly recently, to help the children make the connection between the festivals.)*

Song

Play some of the typical Jewish folk music you chose for the children and teach them the simple circle dance to express their joy, if you have chosen to do so.

SUKKOT
Feast of Tabernacles and Harvest (September/October – movable festival)

By Manon Ceridwen Parry

Suitable for Key Stage 1

Aims

To learn about the festival of Sukkot and think about thankfulness in general.

Preparation and materials

- **Background** The date of this festival changes, but it is usually in October. It begins on the fifteenth day of Tishri, five days after Yom Kippur. It is a joyful festival on which the Exodus story of the 40 years in the wilderness before arriving in the Promised Land is remembered. It has a harvest thanksgiving theme and involves the making of sukkot (booths), recalling the huts built as shelters in the wilderness.
- **Props** You will need materials with which to make a den – a few chairs, blankets or large cardboard boxes, opened up. Also, choose one of the school's favourite harvest songs to sing at the end of the assembly.

Pronunciation notes (local pronunciations may vary):

Sukkot	soo-cot ('soo' as in 'sooty')
Sukkah	soo-ka

Assembly

1. Ask the children, 'Do any of you have a den?' Talk about when you were a child and how you enjoyed making dens or camping outside or even, maybe, hiding under some blankets in the house. Ask, 'What would you need to build a den?'

2. Come up with some answers too – a roof or some kind of shelter, maybe some sides or a wall. How would they make the den look nice? Talk further about your own experience of making dens as a child.

3. Explain that there is a Jewish festival and it involves making dens. Every year, around October, Jewish families celebrate Sukkot, the feast of tabernacles, by building sukkot, which are huts, a kind of a shelter.

4. The festival of Sukkot reminds Jewish people of the 40 years the Israelites spent in the wilderness on their way to the Promised Land. Ask the children if they remember the story of the Jews escaping from Egypt. The Israelites left Egypt because they were not being treated very well and were used as slaves. So in this festival, Jews remember how hard that time was in the wilderness and how wonderful it was to arrive in a beautiful country with all the food, drink and shelter they needed.

   During those 40 years, however, they learned what it meant to have to rely on God for everything because, even in the wilderness, God protected them and gave them enough to live on. It was a very scary time – they were very grateful for every drink and every bit of food they had.

   This makes the festival of Sukkot one of double thanksgiving – for being led out of the desert and for the harvest, so there will be a good and successful supply of food and drink in the months to come.

   Just building a den, though, wouldn't be enough to help them remember those 40 years in the wilderness. They have to eat and drink in their sukkah (the singular form of sukkot, which is plural) and, in some places, they even sleep in them as well. Ask the children if they would like to sleep in their dens. Probably not! Staying in their sukkah is a reminder of how lucky they are now to have much more than a flimsy shelter to live in.

5. To build a sukkah, you need at least three walls, which can be made of anything. Traditionally, the roof has to be made of something organic – that is, something once growing, so preferably branches, but strips of wood or bamboo could be used – but you have to still be able to see the sky (the sun

and the stars) through it and it should be flimsy and temporary, so it serves as a reminder of that time living in dens, without a proper roof over their heads.

6. So as you explain this, build some kind of a structure, maybe using the back of the hall or classroom as one wall (you are allowed to use an existing structure as part of a sukkah). Use two of the chairs either side and put the blankets or cardboard across the top.

7. Explain, too, that this isn't a proper example of a sukkah – remind the children that the roof has to be made from something organic, like leaves or branches, but with blankets or boxes, at least there are gaps in the roof, as in real sukkot.

    Inside proper sukkot, too, the walls are decorated or even have fruit and branches hanging off the ceiling. Maybe during the day, the children can make pictures to put in the den to make it look nice or even go in it to pray or think about all the things they are thankful for.

8. In the synagogue on the festival of Sukkot, Jews have special services, bring four types of branches and recite special prayers. To end the assembly, say that you are going to read a psalm and, as you read, encourage the children to think about all the things they are thankful for.

Time for reflection

Psalm 114
When Israel went out from Egypt,
the house of Jacob from a people of strange language,
Judah became God's sanctuary,
Israel his dominion.

The sea looked and fled;
Jordan turned back.
The mountains skipped like rams,
the hills like lambs.

Why is it, O sea, that you flee?
O Jordan, that you turn back?
O mountains, that you skip like rams?
O hills, like lambs?

Tremble, O earth, at the presence of the Lord,
at the presence of the God of Jacob,
who turns the rock into a pool of water,
the flint into a spring of water.

Prayer
Thank you for everything you give us – food to eat, clothes to wear and homes to live in. Help us to be grateful always.
Amen

Song

Sing the harvest song you chose in preparation.

HANUKKAH
Festival of Lights
(December – movable festival)

By Manon Ceridwen Parry

Suitable for whole school

Aims

To learn about the festival of Hanukkah and think about what a miracle is for us today.

Preparation and materials

- **Background** Hanukkah (can also be spelt Chanukkah) is the Jewish festival of lights. 'Hanukkah' is the Hebrew word for consecration and celebrates the rededication of the temple in Jerusalem in 165 BC after its desecration by the Seleucid (Greek) Empire of Syria, which was the first Hanukkah. It is held in December and lasts for eight days from the twenty-fifth day of Kislev. Although it occurs at a similar time to the Christian festival of Christmas, there is no connection between them, even if the theme of light is similar and some Christmassy practices have crept into Hanukkah celebrations, especially for those Jews who live in countries where the culture is predominantly Christian. The story can be found in the Bible in the apocryphal books of the Maccabees.
- **Props** Eight candles and means to light them, and a menorah, if you have one. Also, relighting birthday candles and some water in a jug, to put them out! Some of the special foods of the festival can also be used as visual aids – such as latkes (potato pancakes) and doughnuts – though this is optional.

Pronunciation notes (local pronunciations may vary):

Hanukkah	hann-a-ka (nice glottal 'H')
Seleucid	sell-oo-sid
menorah	men-or-a

Assembly

1. Talk about the festival and its origins – that it celebrates the defeat of the Seleucid (Greek) Empire of Syria, which wouldn't allow the Jewish people to celebrate their religion. This happened about 165 BC.

   The Greeks had been sacrificing pigs in the temple at Jerusalem and put up a statue to the Greek God Zeus there. This was very upsetting to the Jewish people as it went against everything they believed in, but the Greek empire was defeated and the Jews were able to get their temple back.

   After the things the Greeks had done in the temple, the Jewish people had to make it clean and special again. So a new altar was made, with new holy objects, and they had a ceremony to rededicate the temple to God. 'Hanukkah' is the Hebrew word for 'consecration', which means to make holy, so this was the first Hanukkah. There was a problem, though – they only had enough olive oil to burn for one day. Then a miracle happened: the oil burned for eight days. So this festival, the festival of lights, celebrates this miracle too. Because oil is important to this festival, special foods cooked with oil are eaten, such as doughnuts and latkes, which are potato pancakes. You can show these foods at this point if you have them.

2. Light the relighting birthday candles. Get a volunteer to come and blow them out (maybe someone whose birthday is around this time). They will find that they can't blow them out – they keep relighting. They are magic candles.

3. Ask the children, 'Are they really magic?' Someone will have invented these candles to make them work in this strange way. Sometimes we don't understand why things seem to go against the rules of nature. Often there will be an explanation – the maker of the candles would be able to explain how they work – but sometimes there is not. As human beings, we don't know everything there is to know about everything. What we don't understand and can only be explained as a work of God is called a 'miracle' – a bit like the miracle of the oil at the first Hanukkah.

Time for reflection

Light the eight candles slowly, one by one. Do not use the menorah, though (just show it to the children if you have one, explaining what it is), out of respect for the different special prayers that are used when lighting the candles in it at Hanukkah.

Encourage the children to think about the freedom we enjoy to worship how we want, whatever our faith, and how we can respect each other more. Maybe, as each of the eight candles is lit, you could, in turn, name eight values present in the festival of Hanukkah that you and the children would like to show in your lives – namely, love, respect, acceptance, friendship, celebration, fun, sharing, light.

Prayer
Help us to love and respect other people, to accept them even if their ways are different, show friendship to people like us and people who are not the same as us, celebrate our own traditions and have fun, share and show light in our lives.
Amen

Song

'Give me oil in my lamp' (*Come and Praise*, 43).

TU BI-SEBAT
New Year of Trees (January/February – movable festival)

By Emma Burford

Suitable for whole school (script suitable for Years 3 to 6)

Aims

To explain the Jewish holiday of Tu bi-Sebat using a play and encourage understanding of different religious ceremonies.

Preparation and materials

- **Background** Tu bi-Sebat is a minor Jewish festival and spellings of its name vary. 'Tu' means the fifteenth day of Sebat, which is the eleventh month of the Jewish calendar. It was an important date in biblical times as it was used to calculate the age of trees and, thus, the time for tithing their fruit. In the Bible (Leviticus 19.23–25), God commanded that when the Israelites came to the Promised Land and planted trees, the fruit from the trees should not be eaten for the first three years the trees were growing. In the fourth year, the fruit was to be set aside for God and, in the fifth year, they could eat the fruit.
- **Props** You will need either the following fruits or pictures of them: grapes, figs, dates, pomegranates and olives.
- **Staging ideas** Split the performance space into three areas. The middle area can be used for the trees and animals, the two areas either side by the spirits, Hillel, Leviticus and the Orlah.
- **Costume ideas** The costumes can be as complicated or simple as you would like! The children could simply wear coloured T-shirts with their role written on the front, or whole animal, tree and spirit costumes could be created. All the spirits, including Hillel and Leviticus, would be from the forest, so they can be in green, but again, you can make your own interpretations. Note, too, that all the children can take part – as extra non-speaking trees or animals.

- **Links with art** The tree costumes could be created by making many green hand prints, in different shades to distinguish between the fruits.
- **Music** Find the song 'Etz Chayim' ('Tree of life') to play at the end of the assembly (there are lots of examples of this hymn online – all in Hebrew, but many with English subtitles). Also, a Shalom song, available at <www.users.zetnet.co.uk/mlehr/reflec/shalom/shalom.htm>.
- To ascertain the date of Tu bi-Sebat, visit <www.bbc.co.uk/religion/tools/calendar>.

Pronunciation notes (local pronunciations may vary):

Tu bi-Sebat	two bish-vat
Seder	seed-er
Orlah	or-la
Hamisha Asar	ham-ee-sha a-sar
Shevat	shou-vat ('shou' as in 'should')
Mishnah	mish-na
Nisan	nigh-san
Elul	e-lul
Tishri	tish-ree
Shevat	she-vat (with short 'e')
Hillel	hill-el

Editor's note: Although grapes grow on vines, not trees, they are celebrated along with the other fruits, so we have included grape as one of the 'trees' for the sake of dramatic consistency.

Assembly

1. Ask the children to identify what the following fruits are: grapes, figs, dates, pomegranates, olives. Where do they grow?
2. Tell the children watching the assembly that today they are going to learn about the Jewish festival of Tu bi-Sebat from a book in the Bible, Leviticus. They will learn that Jewish people eat these and other fruits as part of Seder, which is a special symbolic meal celebrated as part of the Tu bi-Sebat festival. They will learn all this by watching a play set in an imaginary forest. The children then perform the play, using the script that follows. You will need children to be the following members of the cast:

Narrator	*Forest spirits*
	Spirit 1
The trees	Spirit 2
Pomegranate	Spirit 3
Olive	Spirit 4
Fig	Spirit 5
Grape	Spirit 6
Date	Spirit 7
The animals	Hillel the Elder
Monkey	Leviticus
Deer	
Rabbit	*Orlah spirits*
Snake	Orlah 1
Owl	Orlah 2
Frog	Orlah 3

The trees' New Year

Narrator: It is *(insert correct date for Tu bi-Sebat that year)* and, in the forest, the fruit-bearing trees were waking. Little did they know that it was a special day.

Pomegranate (Waking up): Ahhhhhh! Oh, the sun's up I see. A wonderful *(insert correct month for Tu bi-Sebat)* morning.

Olive: I had the most wonderful dream last night, Pomegranate. All my leaves were made of gold and I was . . .

Fig (Grumpily waking up): Huh, another dream about gold leaves, eh, Olive? I don't know why you *always* get the dream about your golden leaves.

Grape: It's nice to see someone is in a good mood this morning! Really, Fig, you'd think that on a morning like this . . .

Pomegranate: A wonderful sunny morning.

Grape: Exactly. That you would rise with a smile and let the morning sun warm your frosty leaves and branches.

Date: I quite agree, Grape.

Fig: Don't you all start on me before I've even properly woken up! I was just saying that being a tree and standing constantly next to someone who constantly dreams about having golden leaves can be a bit tedious!

Date: Oh, ignore him! Don't you love being a tree, Fig?

Fig: I do feel it's a lot of standing around!

Grape: Well, I have to admit, being a tree can sometimes make you feel, I don't know, insignificant.

Fig: I wish I was a fir tree, then I could be chopped down and dressed in tinsel and admired for the winter season.

Date: Then you'd miss all the other beautiful seasons we have!

Fig: Other seasons? Wonderful! Worms wriggling around, tickling my roots, rain on my leaves, weighing me down.

Olive: But it doesn't always rain! Besides, if we didn't have rain we wouldn't survive.

Pomegranate: And we *are* fruit-bearing trees. Surely that's much better than being a fir tree for one single celebration.

(Monkey and Deer enter with excitement.)

Monkey: Celebration! So you already know about the celebration! I'm glad you did, I was coming over to wish you a happy New Year, fruit-bearing trees!

Deer: Yes, happy New Year!

Grape: Happy New Year?

Olive: Oh, I love celebrations!

(Rabbit and Snake enter.)

Rabbit: Happy New Year, fruit-bearing trees!

Snake: I s-s-s-uppose you must all be feeling rather s-s-special.

Date: Pomegranate, what month did you say we were in?

Pomegranate: *(Insert correct month)* – it's *(insert correct date for Tu bi-Sebat)*.

Olive: The animals are saying Happy New Year!

Fig: I knew I should have stayed asleep! Everyone's gone mad!

Rabbit: No, we're not talking about the Happy New Year you say at midnight on the thirty-first of December.

Monkey: We mean the New Year of trees!

Olive: New Year of trees?

Fig: Told you – everyone's gone mad!

Pomegranate: I must say, animals, I have never heard of the New Year of trees.

Snake: It's the Jewish festival of Tu bi-Sebat.

Deer: Which is the New Year of trees.

(Everyone starts to talk excitedly about the day.)

Fig: Now, wait a second! *(Everyone stops talking and looks at Fig.)* Before we all start celebrating a day that all us trees know nothing about, I would like to know a little more, if you please.

Monkey: Well, Owl told us all about this Jewish festival.

Deer: Tu bi-Sebat occurs on the fifteenth day of the Hebrew month of Sebat.

Snake: 'Tu' stands for the Hebrew letters Tet and Vav, which are 6 and 9.

Rabbit: Which, added up, makes 15.

Deer: The second part, 'bi-Sebat', is a name used for hundreds of years that represents 'Hamisha Asar BiShvat', which means the fifteenth of Sebat.

Rabbit: Now, the festival is commonly known as Tu bi-Sebat.

Date: Who knew Owl was so knowledgeable?!

(Owl enters.)

Owl: Did someone mention my name?

Olive: We are learning about the New Year of trees.

Date: We did not know it existed.

Owl: Oh, but it does and it is a great tradition in the Jewish faith.

Fig: Hang on a minute, Owl. I have read the Torah in my time as a young seed and I never heard of the Jewish holiday of Tu bi-Sebat.

Owl: Well, my friends, I know of a very wise friend who can explain this.

(Frog enters slowly.)

Grape: Frog? What are you doing here?

Pomegranate: You are the wise friend who can explain about the holiday of Tu bi-Sebat?

Fig: . . . and explain why it isn't in the Torah?

(The trees laugh at Frog.)

Frog: Actually, I can, fruit-bearing trees. The Jewish festival of Tu bi-Sebat is not in the Torah.

Fig: Told ya!

Frog: It is actually in the Mishnah, which was the first written text that collected all the many Jewish oral traditions that were not written in the Torah.

Owl: It was called the Oral Torah, which means the spoken and heard Torah, and, according to Jewish tradition, was given by God orally to Moses in conjunction with the written Torah, which was passed down through the ages.

Date: How wonderful.

Monkey: This tradition of Tu bi-Sebat is one of four New Years in the Jewish calendar in the Mishnah.

Frog: The spirits of the forest will tell us about the four New Years.

Narrator: Then, before the animals and trees, wonderful spirits appeared to show them the four New Years of the Jewish calendar in the Mishnah.

(Forest spirits enter and create still pictures of each of the New Years, as they are described below.)

Spirit 1: The first of Nisan!

Spirit 2: The New Year for kings and festivals!

Spirit 3: The first of Elul!

Spirit 4: New Year for animal tithes!

Deer: Animal tithes?

Frog: A certain number of animals in your herd were given to the priest.

Owl: During the first of Elul, Jewish people also visited the graves of loved ones throughout the month in order to remember and honour those people from the past.

Spirit 5: The first of Tishri!

Spirit 6: New Year for planting and sowing!

Spirit 7: The first of Sebat!

Pomegranate: The New Year of trees! Well, I have to say, I'm feeling quite important!

Frog: You should! It was the great Hillel the Elder who decided that the New Year of trees should be on the fifteenth day of Sebat instead of the first.

Olive: Hillel the Elder?

(Hillel enters.)

Hillel: Yes, I am Hillel the Elder. I was born in Babylon and died in Jerusalem in AD 10. I was a very famous Jewish religious leader. I lived in Jerusalem at the time of King Herod and the Roman Emperor Augustus. I lived a long life of 120 years and, during that time, I studied and taught the Jewish faith. I helped develop the Mishnah and it was my experience and teachings of the Jewish faith that lead the rabbis to agree with me that the fifteenth of Sebat would be the date for calculating the growth, planting and sowing of trees and fruits in accordance with the biblical tithes of Orlah.

(Hillel freezes in position.)

Fig: Now you've lost me again! Biblical tithes? Orlah? What do they have to do with fruit and us?

Date: Really, Fig, you are so impatient!

Monkey: Ooooo! I know this!

Owl: Carry on, Monkey.

Monkey: Well, there are some rules that the Jewish people follow when it comes to eating, and Orlah helps them to know when to eat fruit from the fruit-bearing trees.

Olive: Oooooooo! That means us!

Grape: Remember, Olive, this New Year is all about us!

Olive: I know, it's so exciting!

Monkey: Can I carry on?

Date: Sorry, you may gather that Olive gets excited about . . .

Pomegranate: . . . everything!

Monkey: Well, I was going to impress you more by asking the Orlah spirits to tell you themselves.

(The Orlah spirits appear.)

Orlah 1: We are the fruit of the first three years.

Orlah 2: We are a tradition that is kept in the Jewish faith. The Jewish people use our law in their daily lives and especially in Tu bi-Sebat.

Orlah 3: To understand what we are, take a look at Leviticus, chapter 19, verses 23 to 25 (NRSV).

Leviticus: When you come into the land and plant all kinds of trees for food, then you shall regard their fruit as forbidden; for three years it shall be forbidden to you; it must not be eaten. In the fourth year all their fruit shall be set apart for rejoicing in the LORD. But in the fifth year you may eat of their fruit, that their yield may be increased for you: I am the LORD your God.

Orlah 1: We are the fruit you cannot eat.

Orlah 3: We are not Kosher according to Jewish Law.

Fig: If food is Kosher, that means it is fit for Jewish people to eat as it follows Jewish dietary law.

Orlah 2: In the fourth year, the fruit is to be taken to the temple and eaten there as an offering of thanks to God.

Orlah 1: In the fifth year the fruit can be sold and shared by all.

(The Orlah spirits, Leviticus, Hillel and Forest spirits all exit.)

Snake: This-s-s-s is done during the Tu bi-Sebat seder. The Jewish people eat fruits, ones-s-s-s traditionally from Is-s-s-rael.

Deer: Ones honoured in the Torah.

Fig: Huh, bet they won't be us!

Rabbit: Don't be silly, you are all mentioned in the Torah! Pomegranate, Grape, Date, Olive and even you, Fig. Your fruits are eaten in plenty at the Tu bi-Sebat seder.

Frog: Yes, you are honoured and the tradition of Tu bi-Sebat is still strong today.

Pomegranate: How do we know whether our fruits are Kosher or not?

Frog: This is why the New Year of trees is honoured. Each year on the fifteenth of Sebat, your owners know how old you are and when to share your fruit in accordance with the Jewish traditions and lessons from the Torah.

Olive: So this is almost like our birthday?

Owl: In Jewish Law it *is* your birthday!

Grape: Well, what'll you know?!

Pomegranate: There we were thinking that it was just a normal *(insert day Tu bi-Sebat is celebrated on that year)*!

Fig: I have to say, after today's lesson from our friends the animals and everyone, I do feel honoured to be a fruit-bearing tree after all!

Time for reflection

Take a moment to reflect on the play.

> *Prayer*
> Help us to understand and learn about the festivals of religions all over the world, so that we may respect and honour them.
> **Amen**

Song

Play the 'Etz Chayim' ('Tree of life') and Shalom songs.

8
SIKHISM

BIRTHDAY OF GURU NANAK
Celebration to remember teaching of equality (October/November – movable festival)

By Helen Redfern

Suitable for Key Stage 1

Aim
To learn about equality.

Preparation and materials

- **Background** Guru Nanak (1469–1539) was the founder of the Sikh religion. The birthday of Guru Nanak is traditionally celebrated in the month of Kartik, which is in October or November. This assembly could be used at any time during this period.
- **Props** A gift bag containing party clothes, a hooter, party hat, 'Happy Birthday' banner, CD, fairy cake with birthday candle and means to light it. Also, a picture of Guru Nanak (visit <www.allaboutsikhs.com> and <www.sikhs.org> for examples).

Pronunciation notes (local pronunciations may vary):

Nanak	na-nack
Kartik	car-tick
Gurdwaras	gird-wa-ras

Assembly

1. Everyone is different. Just take a look around you. Can you see anyone who is exactly the same as you? No. Some of us are tall. Some of us are short. Some of us have brown hair. Some of us have blond hair. Some of us are boys. Some of us are girls. There is no one else who is exactly the same as you in this school. In fact, there is no one else who is exactly the same as you in the whole world. What's even more incredible is that there has never been and never will be anyone who is exactly the same as you. That's amazing, don't you think?

2. There is one thing that we all have in common though. Each year, we all have a birthday. Is that right? Let me just check: is there anyone here who does not have a birthday every year? That's what I thought. We all have a birthday. *(Start getting the objects out of the gift bag and putting them on the table.)* We often get new party clothes, and birthday parties would not be the same without hooters, hats and banners. We love to sing and dance to our favourite CDs at parties. Then, of course, there is the cake – complete with candles so we can make a wish as we blow them out.

3. Every year at around this time, Sikhs celebrate the birthday of this man – Nanak *(show the picture of him)*. He lived about 500 years ago and yet his birthday is still celebrated every year. Let's find out why.

    Nanak was born into an ordinary family in an ordinary village in what is now Pakistan in 1469. Like most young children, he was very inquisitive and asked lots of questions. As a boy, he looked after the family cattle and would enjoy discussing life with Muslim and Hindu holy men who lived in the forests around the village. Nanak got married when he was 16 and had two sons. He worked as an accountant by day and enjoyed poetry, singing and making music in his free time.

    Then, everything changed. This ordinary man changed. God appeared to Nanak. This ordinary man left his job and gave everything he had to the poor. He travelled far and wide, telling people what God had revealed to him. When he became old, people travelled great distances to hear him teach in his home. This man became known as a 'guru', which means a great teacher.

    The message God gave him was simple. It was that God created everyone and God loves everyone. God sees all of us as equals – young or old, rich or poor, male or female, Hindu or Muslim – and wants us all to treat each other as equals. This was a difficult message at that time as Hindus and Muslims were constantly arguing and fighting over religious issues. It is still a difficult message to remember today.

4. All those who follow Guru Nanak's teaching today are called Sikhs. He is very important to them as he was the founder of the Sikh religion. That is why they celebrate his birthday every year with great joy and enthusiasm. In the Punjab region in India, children are given new clothes *(hold up the party clothes)* and have the day off from school to join in the celebrations.

There are often processions through the streets led by religious leaders. They are followed by school bands *(blow the party hooter)* and people dressed in mock battle costumes *(hold up the party hat)*. The route is adorned with flags, flowers, banners *(hold up the party banner)* and gateways are decorated to depict various aspects of Sikhism. In the Sikh temples, which are called gurdwaras, the Sikh holy book, called the Guru Granth Sahib, is read from beginning to end. This is followed by singing *(hold up the party CD)*, teaching and poetry. Everyone shares a meal provided by a free kitchen in the temple – special food *(hold up the fairy cake with the candle in it)* is eaten and served to everyone there. Candles are lit *(light the candle)* in the Sikh temples and in homes, shops and offices. Firework displays go on late into the night *(blow out the candle)*. It sounds like quite a party, doesn't it?!

5. Sikhs remember the birthday of Guru Nanak every year because he was a very special person with a very special message. Let us take a few moments now to remind ourselves of his message.

Time for reflection

Whether you are a boy or a girl, God created you.
Whether you are young or old, God cares for you.
Whether you are rich or poor, God loves you.

Whatever religion you follow, God created you.
Whatever country you were born in, God cares for you.
Whatever you can and can't do, God loves you.

Just as Guru Nanak did, we can choose to live out this message in our own lives today.

We can choose *not* to laugh at those who are different.
We can choose to be kind.

We can choose *not* to argue with those who are different.
We can choose to bring peace.

We can choose *not* to look down on those who are different.
We can choose to treat everyone as equals.

Just before we go, take another look around you.
Yes, we are all different, but we are also all equal.

Song

'God knows me' (*Come and Praise*, 15)

HOLA MOHALLA
Celebration of valour and defence preparedness
(March – movable festival)

By Helen Redfern

Suitable for Key Stages 1 and 2

Aim

To explore valour and defence preparedness – being brave and prepared.

Preparation and materials

- **Props** Four cards with 'When?', 'Why?', 'How?' and 'What?' written on them, plus four volunteers to hold the cards. For the part of the assembly devoted to 'How?', it is good to have pictures of or, even better, the following: swords and shields, hobby horses or riding hats, musical instruments and poetry book, a history book and a holy book and bowls. If you have the objects themselves, then you can invite children to act out the festival. Visit <www.allaboutsikhs.com> for information and pictures.
- To ascertain the date of Hola Mohalla, visit <www.bbc.co.uk/religion/tools/calendar>.

Pronunciation notes (local pronunciations may vary):

Hola Mohalla	ho-la ma-halla
Phalguna	fal-goo-na
Anandpur	an-and-pour
Gobind	go-bind ('bi' as in 'bin')
Granth	graanth

Assembly

1. In this assembly, we are going to find out about Hola Mohalla. Is it the latest dance craze? Is it a type of curry? Is it an exotic

beach destination for the rich and the famous? No, it is an important Sikh festival and we are going to discover more by asking these four questions. *(Ask your volunteers to hold up each of the four question cards in turn.)*

2. *(For the 'When?' card.)* When does the festival of Hola Mohalla take place? Well, Hola Mohala is celebrated in the month of Phalguna in the Sikh calendar. It takes place every year on the day after Holi, which is a religious festival celebrated by Hindus. The festival is held at the Sikhs' holy city of Anandpur Sahib, in the Punjab, and all round the world. It is a movable festival and, in *(insert current year)*, it takes place on *(insert date for this year's festival)*, lasting from three days up to a week.

3. *(For the 'Why?' card.)* Why does the festival of Hola Mohalla take place? It was established by the last of the Sikh leaders, Guru Gobind Singh, in his lifetime. At that time, the Sikh people were being attacked by those around them and Guru Gobind Singh organized them into a community of soldier-saints to protect and defend themselves. The Sikh soldiers stood together, united in their bravery and were able to withstand the onslaught of a mighty enemy. This festival became a gathering of Sikhs to take part in military exercises and mock battles to remind them of the need for 'valour and defence preparedness' (remember these words).

4. *(For the 'How?' card.)* How does the festival of Hola Mohalla take place? Well, this is where the fun begins: this great festival lasts for three whole days.

5. *(Invite children to come up, and give out the props so that they can act out each of the activities described below in turn as you mention them, then freeze in position when you move on to the next one.)*

- Mock battles are held and people dress up in colourful costumes, carrying long shiny spears and swords. They pretend to fight like the Sikh army would have fought its battles many years ago. There is also a parade of Sikh martial arts. *(The children hold the swords and shields and pretend to fight.)*
- There are great displays of horse riding, where people gallop past the crowds at great speed. They also perform daring stunts riding bareback, even standing upright on

two speeding horses. *(The children perform mock stunts and galloping using the hobby horses or wearing the riding hats.)*
- Music and poetry competitions take place to find the best musicians and poets in the land. *(The children pretend to play the musical instruments and read from the poetry books.)*
- Stories are told of the amazing bravery of Guru Gobind Singh and passages are read from the Sikh holy book, the Guru Granth Sahib. *(The children pretend to read from the history and holy books.)*
- All the visitors to the area are invited to share in a traditional meal prepared and provided by the local people. *(The children pretend to eat the imaginary food in the bowls.)*

6. Just imagine how much fun it is to be at this festival with all these activities going on. *(Encourage the children to all act out their parts together.)* What a fantastic celebration! *(Thank the children, then ask them to go and sit down in the audience once more.)*

7. *(For the 'What?' card.)* So, finally, what can the festival of Hola Mohalla remind us of today? Guru Gobind Singh wanted Sikhs to remember the importance of two things: valour and being prepared to defend themselves. What do these two concepts mean for us today? What does 'valour' mean? It means courage or bravery. It means standing up for what is right even when you are afraid. It means overcoming your fear and doing the right thing. What does 'being prepared' mean? Being prepared to defend the truth. Being prepared to stand up for the weak. Being prepared to stand by your friends.

Time for reflection

Let us finish this assembly by reflecting on these two concepts – being brave and being ready – and combine them in a question: 'Are you ready to be brave?'

When your friends start picking on the new kid in the playground, are you ready to be brave and stand up for what is right?

When your teacher is trying to find out the truth about an incident in the classroom, are you ready to be brave and tell the truth?

When you see an old person struggling with some shopping bags, are you ready to be brave and lend a helping hand?

When you hear people make unkind comments about people who are different from them, are you ready to be brave and stand up for equality?

When you see other children dropping rubbish on the ground, are you ready to be brave and set a good example?

When we remember what we have learnt about the festival of Hola Mohalla, let us remember to be ready to be brave, any time, any place, any day.

Song

'He who would valiant be' (*Come and Praise*, 44)

BAISAKHI
Sikh New Year and celebration of commitment (13 April)

By Helen Redfern

Suitable for Key Stage 2

Aim

To value commitment.

Preparation and materials

- **Background** Baisakhi, also spelt Vaisakhi, is the celebration of the Sikh New Year and falls on 13 April. It also recalls the institution of the 'Khalsa' in 1699 after a long period of Sikh persecution. Guru Gobind Singh, the tenth and last human guru (the Sikh holy book, Guru Granth Sahib, is considered to be the final guru), called together all the Sikhs and instituted a group of five men known as the Khalsa who would be willing to die for God, if necessary, defend their faith and care for the poor and helpless. Ever since, men and women from as young as 16 or 18 have been initiated into the Khalsa as a sign of their commitment to following the Sikh way of life. On Baisakhi, people gather in gurdwaras (temples), where there is a continuous reading of the Guru Granth Sahib. The flagpole is washed and a new Sikh flag is put in place. There are also shared meals and celebrations. Very often, people are initiated into the Khalsa on this day. Visit <www.allaboutsikhs.com> for more information.
- **Props** Four cards with 'Sport' written on the first, 'Faith' on the second, 'Learning' on the third and 'Creativity' on the fourth. You will need four volunteers to hold the cards. You will also need one more card with the word 'Commitment' on it.

Pronunciation notes (local pronunciations may vary):

Gobind	go-bind ('bi' as in 'bin')
Baisakhi	buy-sack-i

Assembly

1. Explain to the children that you are going to tell the story behind this festival, which is very important to Sikhs.

The Khalsa

Imagine the scene. You are standing with the rest of your people in an open area surrounded by your enemies on all sides. It is 1699 and your people have suffered for many years. You all feel defeated, weak, helpless and without hope. Your leader stands up to speak – a hush descends over the whole crowd. What could he say to encourage you now? Thousands of faces turn to look expectantly at this leader, this Guru, feeling nervous and excited at the same time.

'I need a Sikh who is willing to die for the God of his people.'

What? What is he saying? He needs someone willing to die for God?

'I need a Sikh who is willing to die for the God of his people.'

Has he gone mad? Surely nobody wants to die. That was why they had all gathered here today.

'I need a Sikh who is willing to die for the God of his people.'

Your eyes scan the crowd, looking to see if anyone will volunteer. Everyone is looking at their feet. No one is moving, but, wait – one man steps forward and enters the tent with the Guru.

Now everyone is whispering, wondering what is going to happen. Then here comes the Guru, all by himself, with a sword covered in blood in his hand! The Guru speaks again.

'Who is now willing to sacrifice himself for God?'

Everyone is in shock, horrified. Has the Guru killed the man? Surely no one else would volunteer now, but then another man steps up and goes into the tent with the Guru.

Again, the Guru comes out alone, with a sword covered in blood. You cannot believe your eyes. All the same, another man goes forward – then another. This happens five times. Five times the Guru comes out alone with blood on his sword.

What is this? There is movement at the entrance to the tent. All five men come out alive! The Guru lifts his hand and silence falls. He speaks and everyone listens.

'This was a test to see who would be brave enough and willing to give up everything to show how much they are devoted to God.'

Wow! A test! You cannot believe your ears. You have never seen such devotion, such commitment. You know in your heart that this special day will always be celebrated by your people.

2. The leader in the story was Guru Gobind Singh, the tenth and last human guru of the Sikh religion. The five men who volunteered became the first members of a group called the Khalsa, which defends the Sikh faith and cares for the poor and helpless. What happened on this special day is still remembered every year by Sikhs on 13 April. It is called Baisakhi and is also Sikh New Year, celebrated by Sikhs all over the world. On this special day, too, men and women as young as 16 are initiated into the Khalsa. They make a commitment to the Sikh way of life, just as those five men did so dramatically all those years ago.

3. For each of us, commitment is an important part of life. We have to show commitment to the activities that we are involved in. Let us consider some examples. *(Invite your four volunteers to come up to the front to, in turn, hold the four cards you prepared.)*

(For the 'Sport' card.) Maybe you play football or netball. Maybe you love gymnastics or swimming. How would someone show commitment to his or her sport? *(Invite suggestions, if you feel comfortable with that, but here are some examples of the kinds of answers you would expect:*
- *stay healthy by eating the right food and exercising*
- *turn up to training even if you don't feel like it*
- *listen to the coach and try your hardest to do what he or she advises.)*

(For the 'Faith' card.) Maybe you are a Sikh or a Christian. Maybe you are a Hindu or a Muslim or belong to another faith. How would someone show commitment to his or her faith? *(Invite suggestions, if you feel comfortable with that, but here are some examples of possible answers:*
- *find out more about your faith from your leaders and your holy book*
- *meet regularly with people who share your faith*
- *learn to live your life by the rules of your faith.)*

(For the 'Learning' card.) Maybe you are interested in maths or fascinated by science. Maybe you love literacy or history. How would someone show commitment to his or her learning? *(Invite suggestions, if you feel comfortable with that, but here are some examples of possible answers:*
- *try your hardest in lessons, even when the work is difficult*
- *do the homework that is set every week*
- *listen to your teacher.)*

(For the 'Creativity' card.) Maybe you love singing or dancing. Maybe you are good at art or playing the piano. How would someone show commitment to his or her creativity? *(Invite suggestions, if you feel comfortable with that, but here are some examples of possible answers:*
- keep practising over and over and over again
- carry on even if your friends say unkind things
- go to rehearsals even if you have something more exciting to do.)

4. This story that we have heard today about Guru Gobind Singh is a remarkable example of commitment. People all around us today also show amazing commitment to their faith, education, sport, work and artistic talent. Look out for examples on the television or in the news in this next week.

Time for reflection

How about you? In what area of your life do you show commitment? Take a moment to think about that question now.

Here are some examples to finish with . . . *(Hold up the card with the word 'Commitment' on it and say the following, pointing to each letter in the word in turn.)*

Commitment is:

Cleaning out the rabbit hutch *before* you watch TV
Opening the holy book for your religion to see what it has to say to you
Memorizing the words to a *whole* song
Making the most of every opportunity
Inspiring yourself to follow your dream
Taking your dog for a walk even when it's raining
Maximizing your potential
Exercising every day
Not making excuses
Taking a turn on the bench as a substitute.

> *Prayer*
> Let us learn to show commitment in all that we do.
> Let us always do our very best.
> Let us be the best we can be.
> **Amen**

Song

'When a knight won his spurs' (*Come and Praise*, 50)

MARTYRDOM OF GURU ARJAN
The consequences of jealousy
(16 June)

By Helen Redfern

Suitable for Key Stage 2

Aim

To recognize the consequences of jealousy.

Preparation and materials

- **Background** Guru Arjan was the fifth Sikh Guru and the first Sikh martyr. For additional information, visit <www.allaboutsikhs.org> and <www.sikhs.org>.
- **Props** You will need to recruit three children to read the different parts on the day. Go through the pieces of text that they will be reading below and give them copies of their parts so that they feel comfortable. You will read the 'Narrator' text below. Finally, you will need a candle and means to light it during the 'Time for reflection' section of the assembly.

Pronunciation notes (local pronunciations may vary):

Arjan	are-jan
Prithi Chand	prith-i chaand
Sulhi	sool-ki
Hargobind	haa-go-bind ('bi' as in 'bin')
Chandu	chan-do
Jahangir	ja-han-gear
Mughal	mo-gul

Assembly

1. Gather your three readers to stand with you and, in turn, read the parts below.

   ### The martyrdom of Guru Arjan
   Narrator: Guru Arjan was born in the country we call India in 1563, the youngest son of the fourth Guru, Ram Das. As he

got older, his father asked him to become the next Guru in the respected line of Sikh leaders. His older brother, Prithi Chand, became very jealous.

Prithi Chand: It's just not fair. I should be the next Guru, not him. I am the eldest son. He has done so many amazing things since he has become our leader. He has laid the foundation of the Golden Temple. He has travelled all over the Punjab and everyone loves him. I'm so jealous. That should be me.

Narrator: So what did jealousy make this older brother do?
- He persuaded Sulhi Khan, a revenue officer of the Mughal court, to raid Amritsar and force Guru Arjan out of town.
- He tried to convince the Sikhs that he was the real guru and not Arjan.
- He came up with a plan to assassinate Guru Arjan's only child, Hargobind.
- He composed his own hymns and pretended to visiting Sikhs that they were written by Guru Nanak and the other Gurus.

A rich arrogant Hindu banker from Delhi called Chandu Shah tried to marry his daughter to the Guru's son, Hargobind, because he was jealous of Guru Arjan's popularity and reputation and wanted to be a part of it. Guru Arjan refused the match.

Chandu Shah: It's just not fair. What right does this Guru have to refuse my daughter's hand in marriage for his son? Who does he think he is? Does he know how rich I am? Does he know how important I am? I am successful in business and yet the only person anyone talks about is him. I'm so jealous. It makes me mad.

Narrator: So what did jealousy make this rich man do? Well, Chandu Shah complained to the Emperor Akbar that Guru Arjan had prepared a book which was derogatory in nature to Muslims and Hindus. The Emperor could not find anything wrong with the holy book that Guru Arjan had compiled, however.

When the Emperor Akbar died, Jahangir became Emperor. He was not a good man and spent all his time living selfishly and drinking. Emperor Jahangir was jealous of the Guru's popularity because he had many followers who were captivated by his teaching.

Emperor Jahangir: It's just not fair. I am the new Emperor. I have all the power and authority, yet everyone is following this Guru wherever he goes. They listen to every word he says. They follow his example. He should not be so popular. I'm so jealous. I will find a way to punish him.

Narrator: So what did jealousy make this Emperor do? To please the Muslims in India, who did not approve of his behaviour, Emperor Jahangir had Guru Arjan arrested. Some say it was because he gave a blessing to a Muslim. Some say it was because he was unable to pay a large fine. Some say it was because he would not change the words in the holy book. Whatever the reason, Guru Arjan was thrown in jail and tortured. He was forced to sit on a red hot iron sheet. Burning hot sand was poured over his body. The Guru was dipped in boiling water. He was tortured in this way for five long days.

Three men were all jealous of Guru Arjan and this is what that jealousy led to.

On 30 May 1606, Guru Arjan asked for a bath in the river Ravi by the side of the Mughal fort. His bare body was covered with blisters. The Guru calmly walked into the river and was gone for ever, his body carried away by the currents.

2. What about you? What does jealousy make you do?
   - Jealousy can make us say unkind and spiteful things.
   - Jealousy can make us try to get someone else into trouble.
   - Jealousy can make us lie and steal and cheat.
   - Jealousy can make us want to hit and hurt someone else.
   - Jealousy can make us spoil someone else's work.

3. Jealousy can have bad consequences. Jealousy can be dangerous if it is left to get out of control. We need to recognize and deal with jealousy as soon as we feel it in our hearts.

4. The anniversary of the martyrdom of Guru Arjan (he died for his faith and the Sikh people) is remembered by Sikhs all over the world every year. It would be good for us all to remember this story and the very real consequences of jealousy every day of our lives.

5. Let us take a few minutes now to reflect on what we have heard today.

Time for reflection

(Light a candle.)

Let's think about times when we've been jealous. About the people we may still be jealous of.

Let's try to overcome that feeling by reflecting on what we have, what we're good at and how much our families and friends like us for who we are, not what we have.

Song

'Lord of all hopefulness' (*Come and Praise*, 52)

9
ZOROASTRIANISM

NO RUZ
Zoroastrian New Year
(21 March – movable festival)

By Gordon Lamont

Suitable for Key Stage 2

Aims

To introduce the Zoroastrian faith and its key festival of No ruz (New Year).

Preparation and materials

- **Background** No Ruz is celebrated on the day of the astronomical vernal equinox (when day and night are the same length), which usually occurs on 21 March.
- **Props** You will need a broom, duster or other cleaning items, a plate of any attractive-looking food, a holy book, such as the Bible, a mirror, a wrapped present, something growing, such as sprouted mustard seeds or a vibrant-looking plant, an incense stick, perfumed candle or any other item that has a pleasing scent, a goldfish in a bowl or an image of one. You will also need one or more candles and means to light them. You could involve your class in gathering all of these items in advance. Alternatively, the children could draw large pictures of each of these things to display at the appropriate points during the assembly. On the day, conceal the items ahead of time in the hall or other room, ready to produce them one by one.

Pronunciation notes (local pronunciations may vary):

>   Zoroastrianism   zoro-astri-an-ism
>   Zoroaster   zoro-aster

Assembly

1. Enter the space as if busy. Produce your broom or duster and start cleaning up, explaining that you'd like to stop and talk but, really, you must get on and have the place clean and

ready for the festival. Dust one or two children (or teachers!) perhaps, and, if time allows, you could enlist some to help you.

2. Produce your plate of food and explain that, of course, you and your friends and family will be sharing a meal together. Ask if anyone has any idea what the festival is? Value all suggestions given by the children. If, by any remote chance, someone does hit on the right answer, respond with, 'We'll see!'

3. Continue to produce the hidden items one by one, each time asking what the festival could be.

4. When you have worked your way through everything you've hidden, explain that the festival is called No Ruz or sometimes Now Ruz or Nooruz, plus other variations! It's from a very old religion called Zoroastrianism founded by the prophet Zoroaster some time in the sixth century BC in a part of the world that we now call Iran. He was one of the very first people to teach that there is one God. It is a thoughtful faith. Its followers are supposed to live a life of good thoughts, good words and good deeds. It is estimated that it is followed by about 250,000 worldwide.

5. Explain that No Ruz is a celebration of the Zoroastrian New Year. Ask the children, 'What do you think is the meaning or purpose of each of the things that I've shown?' The answer is that they are all used in activities that take place in the homes of followers of the Zoroastrian faith during the festival.

   - **Cleaning** to get the house ready and make it 'special'
   - **Food** a celebration meal is prepared, to enjoy each other's company and share it together
   - **Presents** to show love for family and friends
   - **Holy book** to symbolize (help us think about) guidance being given on how to live a good life
   - **Mirror** to think about the past and look to the future
   - **Something growing** to represent new life
   - **Incense** to encourage meditation when we can think about what's important in life
   - **Goldfish** to represent life and activity
   - **Candles** to stand for light, energy and the sharing of warmth.

6. Explain that, over the next two weeks, Zoroastrians will visit friends and neighbours and give each other gifts. If they have upset anyone in the past, they try to put things right during this time by being friendly and helpful.

7. They also build bonfires on the last Wednesday before the festival, as a way of preparing for the festival. That is because fire is seen as a symbol of the light of wisdom, health, goodness and purification. People jump over the fire in celebration and often on these days fireworks are set off too.

Time for reflection

There's a lot we can learn from Zoroastrianism – it's a thoughtful faith, encouraging good thoughts, good words and good deeds.

Think a good thought now – something that you can be happy about and thankful for. Determine that you will say some good words today – what will they be and who will you say them to? What good deed will you do today – something to help other people?

Now we're going to wish each other a Happy No Ruz – Happy Zoroastrian New Year. The words we say to do this are 'No Ruz Mubarak'. Ready? One, two, three – No Ruz Mubarak!

Song

'The best gift' (*Come and Praise*, 59)

ZARTUSHT-NO-DISO
Remembering the first Zoroastrian prophet (26 May/ 26 December – movable festival)

By Gordon Lamont

Suitable for Key Stage 2

Aim

To introduce this Zoroastrian festival and reflect on the teachings of Zoroaster.

Preparation and materials

- **Props** You will need a whiteboard or flipchart to display, in turn, the phrases 'Zartusht-no-diso', 'good thoughts', 'good words' and 'good deeds'. You will also need a candle and means to light it.
- **Music** This is optional, but you could play the theme from the film *2001: A Space Odyssey* – 'Also sprach Zarathustra' ('Thus Spake Zarathustra') by Richard Strauss.
- **Note** As you can see above, the date for this festival varies widely depending on which Zoroastrian calendar is used, so this assembly can be held whenever you like!

Pronunciation notes (local pronunciations may vary):

Zoroastrian	zoro-astri-an
Zoroaster	zoro-aster
Zartusht-no-diso	zar-tusht no-diso (the festival is also known as Zarthost no deeso or Zartusht-no-deeso, so pronunciation varies)

Assembly

1. If you have chosen to play the theme from *2001: A Space Odyssey* – 'Also sprach Zarathustra' – play it now. Ask the children if they've heard it before and, if so, where and when? What does it make them think of, what pictures do they see in their minds as they listen to it? Tell them the title. Explain that

it was used in a famous science fiction film made in 1968: *2001: A Space Odyssey*. The music was inspired by a book of philosophy with this title, the main character in which is 'Zarathustra'.

2. Explain that spellings change over time, but Zoroaster, as he is known, was a prophet and founded the faith named after him – Zoroastrianism – in the area that we now call Iran. He was one of the very first people to teach that there is one God.

3. Explain that Zoroastrianism is a thoughtful belief system. Fire and flame play an important part in Zoroastrian festivals, sometimes with people leaping over bonfires, sometimes with them meditating while focusing on a sacred flame. Zoroastrians do not think that God is a flame, but it represents his light and wisdom, and focusing on something visible but not solid, giving heat and light, can help us think about God.

4. Explain that Zoroaster spent many years meditating on his own in a cave before emerging with his message. Suggest that, although spending so much time meditating might be taking things a bit far, perhaps we could all do with thinking carefully for a moment or two before we act or speak. Ask the children for their ideas about this – what difference would it make to school life? Can they think of any examples?

5. Teach the children the name of the festival, showing the name of it on the whiteboard or flipchart, repeating it several times all together.

    An optional thing you can do at this point, to turn this into a fun game, is orchestrate the children so that the words travel across the room. For example, you could ask for the children on your left to start the process by saying 'Zar', then for the next block to carry it on by saying 'Tusht' and so on. Try going from left to right, right to left, front to back and back to front too, if time allows.

6. Explain that this is the name of a Zoroastrian festival and it commemorates (helps people to remember and think about) the death of Zoroaster. At this time (the date varies depending on tradition and location), Zoroastrians come together to visit the fire temples, pray and meditate on the message of their prophet. They have lectures and discussions to help them think about three important things and we're going to do that now.

7. Reveal the phrase 'good thoughts' on the whiteboard or flipchart and ask the children for their ideas about it. What is a good thought? Do they have any examples?
8. Repeat for the phrases 'good words' and 'good deeds'.

Time for reflection

Light the candle and invite the children to look at it during this time. If you can, darken the room for this part of the assembly.

Recap, saying that there's a lot we can learn from Zoroastrianism – a thoughtful faith, encouraging good thoughts, good words and good deeds.

Tell the children how Zoroastrians find that looking at a flame as they meditate helps them to think about God. Look at the candle and spend a few moments being calm and still, thinking your own thoughts. Don't force ideas into your head, just allow your thoughts to come and go in the silence.

At the end of the time, ask the children to have a day of good thoughts, good words and good deeds.

Song

'Christ be our light' (*Hymns Old and New*, Kevin Mayhew, 2004)

Index

Authors
Barker, Alan 58, 61, 64, 67, 70, 73
Burford, Emma 2, 8, 111
Challis, John 38
Chilcott, Laurence 32, 41, 47, 50
Lamont, Gordon 138, 141
Parkinson, Rebecca 35, 44, 54, 90, 94
Parry, Manon Ceridwen 98, 101, 104, 108
Redfern, Helen 122, 125, 129, 133
Ross, Janice 76, 82, 86
Scrutton, Jude 20, 24, 27, 80
Tuxford, Jenny 13, 16

Bible references
Leviticus 19.23–25 118
Psalm 114 106
Matthew 2.1–12 35

Children's lives
Beavers/Brownies/Cubs/Guides/Rainbows/Scouts 44
birthday (cake) 27, 36
bonfires 140, 142
brothers/sisters/siblings 70, 71
  caring for one another in school holidays 71
  wristbands for 70
cake 87
candles 25, 82, 108, 124, 138
cards 59, 80, 82
community 76–8
  school badge as mark of 76
creativity 129
Elmer the elephant 65
fireworks 59, 124, 129, 140
flags 90, 129

friends/friendship 47, 60, 68, 110, 139
'Green Flag', environmental award 32
happiness 24, 68, 82
homework 14
jealousy 133
learning 129
mealtimes 41
neighbours 78, 139
new beginnings 74, 84
new school 72
perfume/incense 92
presents 27, 35, 36, 84, 139
recycling 32
reduction of waste 32
respect 96, 100, 103
soldiers 54, 126
sport 129
television 88, 132
thankfulness 104
valour 125
welcome 67
see also Religious phrases/vocabulary

Countries/places
Afghanistan 5
Amritsar 134
Anandpur Sahib (Punjab) 126
Assisi 33
Azerbaijan 5
Babylon 117
Baghdad 8, 9, 10, 14
Bahji (Israel) 15
Burma (Myanmar) 20, 27
Cambodia 27
China 27
Constantinople *see* Istanbul
Delhi 134

145

Egypt 105
Germany 47
India 5, 28, 58, 64, 73, 90, 95, 123, 133
Indonesia 27
Iran 2, 5, 8, 13, 15, 17, 139
Istanbul 11
Jerusalem 42, 49, 50, 52, 108, 117
Loyola (Spain) 54
Malaysia 27
Mecca 76
Medina 76
Mount Carmel, Israel 18
Nazareth 45
Nepal 21, 27
Netherlands 47
Japan 20
Pakistan 5, 123
Persia *see* Iran
Rome 33
San Francisco 28
Saudi Arabia 76
Scandinavia 47
Singapore 27
South Korea 20
Sri Lanka 20, 27
Syria 108
Taiwan 27
Tajikistan 6
Tehran 10
Thailand 20, 27
Tibet 20
Tokyo 28
Turkey 5
United States of America 20
Vietnam 27

Culture
2001: A Space Odyssey 141
angels 36
charity 55
conservation 33
demon (Ravana) 59–60
flute 68
food 33, 59, 124, 139
gurdwaras 124, 129
Last Supper, The (Da Vinci) 41
Latin 55
mosques 78, 81, 82, 84, 88
Rapunzel 20
Roman Catholic Church 55
shepherds 36
sustainability 33
synagogues 98, 99, 101, 102, 106
Tangled (Disney) 20
vegetarianism 91
wine 33

Famous people
Abraham 2, 8, 13, 16, 80
Anna 38
Anthony of Egypt 19
Augustus (Roman Emperor) 117
Bab, The 16
Baha' Ullah 2, 8, 13, 14, 16
Buddha 2, 8, 13, 16, 20, 21, 23, 24, 27
  see also Siddhartha Gautama
Francis, St 32
Gurus
  Arjan 133
  Gobind Singh 126, 129
  Nanak 122
  Ram Das 133
Herod 117
Ignatius of Loyola 54
Isaac 80
Ishmael 80
Jesus Christ 2, 8, 13, 16, 34, 35, 36, 38, 41, 42, 45, 47, 50
John the Baptist 45
Judas 48
Magi (wise men) 36
Mary 38
Moses 2, 8, 13, 16, 116
Muhammad 2, 8, 13, 16, 17, 76
Peter 48, 50, 51–2, 53
Siddhartha Gautama 21
Simeon 38

Zarathustra *see* Zoroaster
Zoroaster 2, 8, 13, 16, 141–2

Holy books
Bible 48, 55, 138
Guru Granth Sahib 124, 127, 129
Mishnah 116
Qur'an 78, 84, 87
Torah 115

Music
'Also Sprach Zarathustra' 141
'Etz Chayim' 112
'I see the light' 20, 21
Jewish folk music 103
Shalom songs 119

Nature
animals 32, 93
 bees 74
 butterflies 74
 cows 65, 68, 92
 deer 113
 dog 132
 elephant 61
 frog 113
 goat 81, 98
 goldfish 138
 insects 91
 monkey 113
 owl 113
 rabbit 113
 sheep 81, 98
 snake 113
flowers 14, 15, 73
 roses 15
food
 apples 98
 dates 82, 111
 eggs 74
 figs 111
 fruit 39, 90, 91
 grapes 111
 honey 98
 olives 111
 pomegranate 111
environment 32, 33
 desert 105
 forest 59
 garden 8, 21
 trees 112
 wilderness 104
moon 80, 83
mountains 17, 49
stars 106
sun 15, 87, 105
valleys 17
vernal equinox 2, 138
weather 94
 rain 15, 94
 rainy season 95
 snow 94
 sunshine 94

Religious phrases/vocabulary
enlightenment 20, 22, 27, 91
Eucharist/Holy Communion/Lord's Supper/Mass 41, 43
faith 129
fasting 44, 45, 82, 86–8, 102
incense/frankincense 36, 92, 138
Jesuits 55
Khalsa 129
kindness 84, 103
meditation 19
peace 26, 29, 68, 95
see also Children's lives/culture

Religious themes
Atonement, Day of 101
commitment 132
crucifixion 42, 48
disciples 48, 51
dove (Holy Spirit) 50
fast 22, 44, 82, 94, 101
fire 50, 52
forgiveness 51, 84, 96, 99, 101
grace 56

Holy Spirit 49, 50
humility 86
Judgement, Day of 98, 101
light 50, 58, 108
miracle 108, 109
self-control 86

Seasons
Ash Wednesday 45
Christmas 35, 41, 83, 90, 108
Easter 45, 47, 48, 50, 90
Harvest 52, 64, 104
New Year celebrations
  Baisakhi 129
  Diwali 58
  No Ruz 138
  Rosh Hashanah 98
  Tu bi-Sebat 111
Remembrance 98
Shrove Tuesday 45